THE
FIRST
WOMAN
DOCTOR

The Story of Elizabeth Blackwell, M.D.

Rachel Baker

Inside illustrations by Evelyn Copelman

SCHOLASTIC INC.
New York Toronto London Auckland Sydney

In grateful acknowledgment of the help given to this effort by MRS. FRANK A. VANDERLIP, ALICE STONE BLACKWELL, the New York Infirmary for Women and Children, and the New York Academy of Medicine, especially the Rare Book Room.

ISBN 0-590-44767-X

12 11 10 9 8 7 6 5 4 3   2 3 4 5/9

Printed in the U.S.A.   40

To

JOANNA and COLEMAN

CHAPTER ONE

THREE LITTLE GIRLS IN LONG, GRAY QUAKER-
like gowns, and white dimity bonnets, were walking with
their governess and talking quite seriously.

"When I grow up," said Anna, eldest of the Blackwell
children, and always believed to be the cleverest, "I shall be
a writer." Anna was just a little over ten, and for several
years had been making up verses and songs.

Marion, always dreamy, thought for a moment. "I think,"
she said, "that I'll just read."

The governess smiled. "And ruin your eyes, I'll venture,
Miss Marion! You wouldn't have half so many headaches if
you didn't read so much!"

1

But Elizabeth who was only six, and always tagging along with her two older sisters, came up rather breathlessly.

"I don't know," she said, "what I'm going to be." She put out her lower lip thoughtfully, and as usual took time making up her mind. "But I think," she said, and her expression was serious, "that it will be something hard!"

When this was repeated at home, everyone laughed. Elizabeth, born in 1821, after the death of two other children, was the third daughter of the Blackwell household, and even from babyhood she had had the reputation for being stubborn and determined.

She had to do everything for herself and she had to do it perfectly. When she was quite small she wouldn't let anyone help her with her boot laces or the buttons on her frocks. And in the schoolroom, even the governess would get tired of watching her, sometimes, her head bent over the slate, her lip thrust out, her forehead all screwed up with the effort of making her letters exactly like those in the copybook.

And if the other children had finished before her and had gone out, the sound of their playing coming in through the open window, from the garden behind the house, that did not seem to trouble her at all. She simply couldn't leave until what she had done satisfied her completely.

"I have never seen such determination," said her Aunt Barbara, eldest of the Blackwell sisters and sternest of them all.

"A pity that such spirit should be wasted on a girl!"

It was one of the other aunts speaking. The four maiden sisters of Mr. Blackwell lived with the family and took a deep interest in the children.

Mr. Blackwell, who happened to come in from the sugar refinery which was connected by an open courtyard with the house, overheard this remark and at once, in his vigorous way, took exception to it.

"What difference does it make whether Elizabeth is a girl or a boy?"

He was a tall man with sharp intense features, dark hair combed up in a peak on his forehead, and long, carelessly-cut sidelocks, which gave his face a somewhat poetic expression. A member of the stern Independent church, a faith rather like that of the Quakers, he believed fiercely in equality.

"All human beings," he said, "are equal. Black, white, rich, poor, men, women: even children have their rights!"

Aunt Barbara pursed her lips. She was a very strict disciplinarian, and her look seemed to say that it was fortunate, indeed, that none of the children were around to hear such revolutionary talk.

Mrs. Blackwell, a pretty, mild woman, dressed in a plain gown and cap, after the fashion of the strict Independent church to which the family belonged, bent her head over her sewing. Sometimes her husband's views were too advanced even for her to follow. And where in the world did he get all his energy?

Lectures, meetings, resolutions. His study table was heaped high with pamphlets and tracts. A prosperous businessman, owner of a busy sugar refinery, he had time to be interested in reforms of every kind. He had opposed the slave trade to America, until a law was passed in England, abolishing it. He often took part in meetings held to discuss the low wages and the poor working conditions of mill workers. And he was very much interested in seeing that women should get the same chance for an education as men.

This principle he carried out thoroughly in his own home. Elizabeth had three younger brothers: Samuel, Henry, and Howard; and two sisters: Emily who was five years younger than herself, and Sarah Ellen, who was still in the nursery.

For all these children, boys and girls alike, Mr. Blackwell outlined the same plan of education.

This was very much in contrast to the usual practice of

teaching girls music, embroidery, drawing and a little French, and giving boys Latin, Greek, mathematics, and the other hard subjects thought necessary for a sound education.

The big house on Nelson Street, one of the finest in the port city of Bristol, was connected by an open court with Mr. Blackwell's sugar refinery. Very frequently, he would come in from the refinery, in the white suit that he wore there, and would go directly to the schoolroom, to listen to the children and their lessons.

In Elizabeth he was particularly interested. With her stubbornness and ambition and terrific energy, she was so like himself. He would train her as carefully, he decided, as any boy. She should have every opportunity!

The little girl in her long pinafore and demure cap was taught very strange subjects: history, and mathematics and Latin, and Greek grammar. And the same subjects were taught to her sisters.

"We can't imagine what the girls will do with all the education you are giving them!" This was a criticism he heard not only from the members of his own family, but even from the distinguished visitors who came to the house.

His answer was always calm, "They shall do what they please!"

It was true, most girls spent their lives in waiting, waiting for the husband that would assure them the home they had been trained to take care of. But no one could imagine the Blackwell girls as waiting. They were far too adventurous, and it was the complaint of their mother and of the four maiden aunts that their father encouraged them. The truth was that if he did have to refuse one of their requests, he did it in such a companionable way that it didn't always seem like a refusal.

One day, Elizabeth and her two older sisters pooled their savings, and procured from the stationer's shop a gadget they had longed for—a toy telescope.

They spent hours in the attic trying to look at the sun, and at the first evening stars. But they couldn't see anything at all unusual, because, obviously, it was a cheap and a very poor telescope. But when they trained it over the housetops and towards the horizon, they saw a line of green trees, which Anna exclaimed in excitement, "must be the woods of the Duchess of Beaufort," a very famous landmark about which all of them had heard.

Elizabeth climbed on a chair. She longed to get a closer view of this beautiful forest, and decided, after a conference with her sisters, that the only way to do so would be to climb out on the parapet. This narrow and dangerous little carpenter's balcony ran outside of the house, just beyond the level of the attic windows, and was, by Aunt Barbara's ruling, forbidden territory to the children.

How to get permission, and from whom?

It was decided to address a petition to Papa, in verse. Elizabeth was sent downstairs hurriedly for ink and for paper, and on a corner of a dusty table in the attic, the verse was written. Anna signed her name in a romantic scrolled hand; Marion inscribed herself "Polly," the nickname her father teasingly had given her; and Elizabeth spelled out the letters "Bessie" so carefully that finally her sisters became impatient.

"You take forever," they said.

Of course she couldn't write as well as Anna and Marion. But they seemed to expect it of her, and she tried to make it up to them by carrying the petition down carefully to lay on her father's desk, in the study, where he would be sure to see it when he came in at night from the refinery.

All night they wondered what would happen. The next morning, at the breakfast table, just after family prayers, their father arose, rustled a paper in his pocket, and then read them the answer, his eyes twinkling.

> Anna, Bessie, and Polly,
> Your request is mere folly,

> The leads are too high
> For those who can't fly.
>
> And if I let you go there
> I suppose your next prayer
>
> Will be for a hop
> To the chimney top!
>
> So I charge you three misses
> Not to show your phizes
>
> On parapet wall
> Or chimney so tall
>
> But to keep on the earth—
> The place of your birth.

Everyone laughed, so did the three petitioners. Then their father, in a very deep voice, and with a look of terrible seriousness which they loved, added another verse.

> "Amen," says Papa.
> "Amen," says Mamma.

"Be it so!" says Aunt Bar.

The last line was like the last roll of the organ at church. Everybody by this time was hilarious, and the girls forgot all about their telescope.

Aunt Barbara, who had tried to look severe but couldn't help smiling, was in charge of the bigger children, since their mother was so often busy in the nursery. And this task she seemed to enjoy very much, carrying around with her a little penny notebook with dark covers, which was called the "Black Book."

To get your name into the Black Book meant being shut out from some family privilege, such as being allowed to go in the family carriage to attend the long sessions of the missionary meetings at church. This was quite an occasion, since big baskets of lunch were packed by the cook, and these were tucked into the carriage. In the intervals between sermons, the families would get together in the corridor of the church, for a kind of basket lunch or indoor picnic to which the children looked forward the whole year.

The Blackwells were not a family that believed, like so many well-to-do families, in locking away the children in the schoolroom, to live a life of their own upstairs, while they lived quite another life down below.

When there were guests for dinner, the children were allowed to sit at a little low table in the dining room, and under Aunt Barbara's back-glancing eye, behaved themselves perfectly.

There were certain visitors whom they favored. One of these was a minister, a certain Mr. Burnet of Cork, who was very jolly and kept the long table in an uproar every time he came.

But on the day when he was due for another visit, Elizabeth found herself inscribed in the Black Book. Instead of being allowed to come down to dinner, she was told to go up in the attic and repent of her unmannerly behavior in the schoolroom earlier that afternoon.

She leaned over the bannister, looked longingly down the stairwell, watched the light stream out of the dining room as the servants hurried in and out with their dishes, and felt for a moment that grownups could sometimes be wrong. She didn't feel in the least guilty.

She was always getting into trouble, and this in spite of the fact that she was always, as her mother said, "fighting the devil."

Her mother was very religious, and continually kept a book of sermons by her bedside. And every night she came into the nursery to hear the children's prayers and their confession of the sins they had committed that day.

"But how can I stop being bad?" said Elizabeth, almost desperately.

At the age of ten she was pale, thin, small for her age, but already far more determined and serious than the other children.

"But how . . ." she cried to her mother, "how?"

Then her mother told her that even good men were tempted sometimes, and had to punish themselves in order to overcome their sins.

This idea rather appealed to Elizabeth. Making herself tough and courageous seemed an interesting thing to do. She had read somewhere that sleeping on the floor was a good thing to do if you wanted to harden your body. She decided to try it, and crept out of her bed secretly, to lie on the floor without covers.

But all that happened was a cold in her head and very soon thereafter she devised a new and much harder kind of punishment. She refused at the table those dishes she liked best, and once went without food a whole day, until her head felt as though it were full of air, and her knees were so wobbly, that she was more inclined than ever to lose her temper and snap at people.

So it seemed that this was no way to cure her inclination to sin. She was an odd child, always thinking out things for herself, and devising hard things to do—almost as if she enjoyed testing herself and wanted to find out how strong she could be.

One day she became sick with an attack of intermittent fever, or probably what we would call malaria today. This sickness starts with a terrible chill, and most people pile immediately into bed, cover up with all the blankets they can find, and pile on all the hot-water bottles or bed warmers.

But Elizabeth did no such thing. Instead she paced the hallway outside her room, her hands clenched, her teeth chattering. And when her mother found her, she explained, miserably, that she was going to walk off the chill, that she intended to conquer it.

Of course, she couldn't do any such thing, because after the chill came the fever, which made her feel so hot and weak that she had to go to bed. She lay with her face to the wall.

"It's a physical weakness," she said, and her humiliation at being ill was worse than the illness!

Yet in spite of this sternness with herself, she could be a good nurse, wringing out cold vinegar compresses and steeping camomile tea for her sister Marion when she was sick with one of her headaches.

But she didn't waste much time stroking her sister's hand, on such occasions, and was sometimes accused of showing no sympathy. The truth was that she was independent and didn't have much use for coddling herself, so couldn't understand why other people should desire it.

Moreover, in some ways, she was somewhat like a strong-willed energetic boy. She liked to get things done, and she had no use for showing her feelings.

Her aunts often complained to Mr. Blackwell, that Elizabeth was very unfeminine, showed very little interest in sewing, and none at all in embroidery and mending and knitting, all accomplishments that they felt every lady should cultivate.

But Mr. Blackwell was inclined, always, to take Elizabeth's side. "Let her grow up to do what she wants. I'm certain," he said, "that she's not wasting her time."

And certainly she wasn't, for although Elizabeth might not have been a brilliant student, like her sister Anna, she was far more methodical and determined.

If her father was reminded, over and over again, that it was all very well to educate his daughters, but what in the world would they do with their training, he showed no sign whatsoever of being concerned. There were no professions open to women, true enough, he said, then it was all the more reason for educating his daughters. And he would conclude, "they will have to make their own opportunities!"

In some ways, Mr. Blackwell was a remarkable man. He believed in tolerance for everybody: for the black man, for the underpaid workman, even for the rich Tories who were abusing the people of England, "not because they are cruel," he said, "but because they don't understand better. The heart," he would say, "must be educated!"

And in defense of this idea of tolerance which was really part of his religion, he was willing to risk everything—even his life!

One day there was a riot of laborers in Bristol. Mr. Blackwell was in town, but his family was at Ovelston, their country place, about nine miles from the city, to which they had been removed because disturbances were expected.

There had been a great deal of dissatisfaction among the workingmen, because their hours were long, their wages were poor, and also because, not being property owners, they could not vote. As a result, they could not elect men who might pass the laws to make their conditions better. They wanted parliamentary reform, and went about signing petitions at first, listening to inflammatory speeches, and then finally, by starting fires and rioting, they tried to force the Tories to grant them the privileges they wanted.

In Bristol, the most important port city on the west coast of England, they burned down the town hall and other important buildings. Next they decided to destroy the old and historic churches of the city.

On the steps of the beautiful church of St. Mary Redcliffe, they were met not by the rector of this church, or by any member who attended there. They were met by a man who belonged to another religious group altogether, but who hated violence and destruction so much that he was willing to risk his life in order to stop the mob.

It was Elizabeth's father, Samuel Blackwell, the sugar

refiner and ardent reformer, who spread out his arms against the church doors and barred the way to the rioters.

They could, without question, have trampled him to death, but fortunately something in his eloquence, and the spectacle of the man's courage must have held them. They listened, and they turned back. There was no more burning that day, and to the city, he had become a hero!

But Elizabeth, her mother, and her brothers and sisters had spent a most anxious night at Ovelston, watching from a high hill behind the house, the reddening glow in the sky towards Bristol. Towards morning, and through the whole day they watched, straining their eyes for the sight of a returning carriage or a rider on horseback.

When Mr. Blackwell finally came back, he was tired and discouraged. The violent faces of the rioters had upset him, and the cowardice of the rich men of the city had been equally discouraging.

"That such things should happen in England!" he said.

In Manchester, some time earlier, the rioting had gone so far that the cavalry had to be called out, and a number of people were killed.

"Neither side will listen to reason, now!" said Elizabeth's father. He spoke frequently about his longing to go to America, a longing that grew as it seemed that his own country came nearer and nearer to the brink of revolution.

He talked with returning visitors from America, and went down to the harbor to watch the emigrant ships setting out. A new country, freer, where life would be easier, and a man's ideas understood!

Elizabeth went to bed every night now with the talk of America in her ears, and was torn between the longing to go, and the feeling of loneliness, like an ache, that beset her at the vision of leaving. The walled garden; the pleasant walks down Kingsdown Parade to Sir Richard Vaughan's place with the green-and-gold peacocks proudly preening themselves behind the grilled gates; the roomy old-fashioned farmhouse at Ovelston with the ancient grate and the deep windows under a thatched roof, where she had spent such happy summers; the footstiles in the orchard behind; the brook, the unforgettable view of the dark Welsh mountains she loved. How could they pick up and leave all this and go so far away where everything would be strange, and new, and alien!

Yet in the morning when she awoke, her feeling was quite different, an excitement, a tingling all over her body! Would they go? Could they go? And when?

Of course, Mr. Blackwell had many problems. This she gathered when she heard her parents speaking together sometimes. To whom to sell the business? And how? And for how much? It seemed these discussions would never end.

And yet they ended quite suddenly. A workman, one day, forgot to watch the tremendous refinery fires. There was a blaze in the sugar house, and before the family could realize what was happening, the walls had ignited, the smoke poured out of the roof, and in less than two hours the building with all of its machinery was destroyed!

"We will have to go now," said Aunt Barbara grimly.

Elizabeth crept into her bed, that night, with a feeling of sadness, yet relief. The decision was made.

Actually it wasn't, because the next morning a committee of businessmen waited on Mr. Blackwell. They offered him a loan in any amount necessary for rebuilding his business!

He could remain if he wanted to. Again the children held their breath. Would they go? Wouldn't they? Their father went upstairs to their mother's sitting room, remaining there for what seemed an unbelievably long time. The gentlemen waited in his study.

Then Mr. Blackwell came down. He walked slowly. His face was calm. He closed the study door behind him. "I have decided," he said, "to emigrate to America with my family." He thanked them for kindness. "But I cannot take the loan," he added.

The visitors went out. Mrs. Blackwell came downstairs. She looked as if she had been crying. The next day they began packing. Everyone was bewildered. It was late April, and the gardener who did not know what else to do went on setting out the early spring plants. He came in with his cap in his hand one day.

"A pity," he said to Mrs. Blackwell, "that you won't be here to see the roses come out."

At the last moment, there was the question of whether they should go as they planned in May, or should wait until the end of the summer. Cholera had broken out in the city among the poor Irish immigrants who came each spring across the Irish channel, to wait in Bristol for the boats to America.

Relatives and friends flocked in to discourage the Blackwells, saying that under such conditions it would be dangerous for them to travel. The packing stopped, was begun, stopped again. But when for four days no new cases were reported, the last of the baggage was tied up, the cook prepared the last breakfast, the maids said good-bye, the neighbors waved from the doorways as the carriage went past, and the Blackwells were finally off for America!

It was a big family party that mounted the merchant ship *Cosmo*, in the Bay of Bristol, on a May morning in 1832. There was Elizabeth, now almost eleven, her seven brothers and sisters, her father, her mother, her aunts, and the family nurse and the governess.

As the ship moved out of the harbor, Elizabeth stood at the railing beside her father, and watched the waving crowd on the dock grow smaller and smaller. The towers and chimney and spires of the city seemed to melt, until there was only a blue smudge on the horizon, and then only the clear sky. Even the dark masses of the Welsh mountains which she had always loved and which hung longest in the sky, became thin like smoke and then vanished.

After a while the gulls that had followed the ship, dipping

towards the sails and then wheeling away, disappeared like dots into the sky. Elizabeth felt a sudden strange fullness in her throat, and in her chest a queer emptiness. But her father's hand tightened on hers. He smiled, and they went down to the hold of the ship together, where the others were waiting. . . .

CHAPTER TWO

I THINK," SAID ELIZABETH, "THAT WE SHOULD name this horse Prudence Crandall!"

"And the other one?" It was Marion who spoke. The two girls were waiting in the yard for their father to come out, and take the carriage to the city.

Elizabeth thought for a moment. "I believe," she said, "we will call this one William Lloyd Garrison."

"A rather doubtful honor for the real Mr. Garrison," said their mother who was watching from the doorway.

But Mr. Blackwell, who came out at this moment, interrupted. "On the contrary," he said, getting into the carriage and gathering up the reins, "I think Mr. Garrison would appreciate our sentiments."

The Blackwells, who had been living in New York for two years now, were taking a great interest in the anti-slave movement.

During the winters, in the city, they attended abolitionist meetings and bazaars, signed petitions, circulated resolutions. In the summers, which they spent in a shabby rented farmhouse on Long Island, the girls could not be so active. So the naming of the carriage horses was about all that on a July morning could be done for the cause of anti-slavery.

Everyone in the house thought it was a capital idea. The two new carriage horses should be named after the country's two great abolitionists, after Prudence Crandall, whose home had been burned in Connecticut, because she dared to teach colored children, and after William Lloyd Garrison, the editor of the fiery anti-slave paper, the *Liberator*.

Elizabeth went into the kitchen and stood for a time watching her sister Marion, who was beating up a pudding. She broke the eggs, egg whites and yolks, separating them into two yellow bowls, and then lifted the cover of the honey jar which was almost empty.

"It's a fine thing," said Marion, "to give up the use of sugar as a slave product, but it's not so easy to cook without it!"

Elizabeth shrugged her shoulders. It was easy to go without things, when you felt you were accomplishing something by it.

She remembered the first time her father had come home from hearing Mr. Garrison speak against slavery. How excited he had been as he told them about the meeting, and how he had repeated in his deep eloquent voice the very words that the great abolitionist had spoken. "I am in earnest. I will not equivocate, I will not excuse, I will not retreat a single inch, and I will be heard!"

Mr. Garrison's paper, the *Liberator* was brought home by their father, and lay openly on the dining room table, where visitors could see it. It was not read secretly here as in so many homes.

And very soon after hearing Mr. Garrison speak, Mr. Blackwell had gone to shake his hand, and to offer his most serious services. The two men had taken to each other instantly. And now the much-criticized abolitionist was a frequent visitor in the home of the Blackwells. Tall, thin, with spectacles on his nose, and a high half-moon of a forehead, he had looked so much like a schoolmaster that Elizabeth at first had been disappointed.

But when he took out a volume of Russian poems from his pocket, and gathering the Blackwell daughters about him, began to read, they all listened breathlessly. And after that, whenever he came, the book was drawn out, sooner or later, from his pocket, and the girls gathered around him.

He loved to recite poetry, which he did with unusual feeling. He even influenced Mr. Blackwell to try his hand at verse. The result eventually was a thin volume of poems entitled *Anti-Slavery Rhymes*, by Samuel Blackwell.

Elizabeth was proud of her father's accomplishment, and read the poems over and over again. She was annoyed to hear her mother say, one day, that while the sentiments expressed in the verses were very noble, they would be much criticized, because the abolitionist movement was not at all popular.

"I beg you, Samuel," she said to her husband, "do not endanger yourself in this work."

And in truth, it was dangerous to come out openly against slavery. Only a few days before, on the 4th of July, 1834, there had been a riot in the city when a mob broke up a meeting of the newly-founded American Anti-Slavery Society. Mr. Blackwell, who was a member, had been present, and came home with his coat torn and his stock missing.

His wife was very agitated, especially when she heard that the home of Lewis Tappan, a prominent abolitionist, had been broken into and the homes of several colored families burned to the ground.

But Elizabeth remembered how her father had faced the angry mob on the steps of the church, back in Bristol, and knew that he would never stop doing what he thought was right, no matter how much personal danger it might bring him.

One afternoon, Mr. Blackwell arrived home very early from the city, and brought with him, in a closed carriage, a whole family of anti-slave fugitives. Elizabeth, coming down hurriedly, to help spread the table for tea, found a strange minister, his wife, and their five children, at the table, all looking dishevelled, tired, and very bewildered.

Mr. Blackwell, who was pale and excited himself, told the story of what had happened. The minister, a prominent member of New York's anti-slave society, had preached a sermon to his congregation pleading with them for tolerance. In this sermon he had taken occasion to say "that even our Lord, Jesus Christ, was of darker skin than we are."

Immediately a cry went through the town and a mob gathered, broke in the door of the parsonage, and would have lynched the minister and perhaps injured his family if they had found them at home.

But Mr. Blackwell had been sent for some time before, and had smuggled the family out in a closed carriage.

"Oh, Father!" said Elizabeth. And even Anna, usually calm, was excited.

For three weeks the minister and his family hid in the home of the Blackwells, not stirring from the house lest they be seen by some passing neighbors. To make room for the visitors, Anna, Marion, Elizabeth, and her younger sister Emily, gave up their beds and went to sleep in the attic on quilts laid out on the floor. It was fearfully hot under the roof of the house, and very hard to sleep. But it felt good to suffer for a cause, and it was almost with a feeling of regret that Elizabeth watched the minister's carriage finally go back to the city.

She had a great deal of energy and wished that she could

write and make speeches like Mr. Garrison, or help fugitive slaves to escape as she knew her father was doing.

But there was nothing to do. The summer passed. The family went back to the city to the rented house that they occupied, which had never seemed like a home to Elizabeth. It was tall and narrow, with a dark, cave-like kitchen in the basement, and a meager penned-up garden. Not at all like the roomy comfortable home that the Blackwells had had in England.

Mr. Blackwell's sugar-refinery business, begun with such small funds when the family had arrived in America, had never really prospered, in New York. The girls helped with the housework, and even Elizabeth, who had always disliked sewing, cut out shirts for her brothers and frocks for her two younger sisters, and helped to take care of George, the baby, born soon after the family arrived in America. There was a great deal to do in a household with nine children. Anna, the eldest, was nineteen now, and Elizabeth, just fourteen, looked grown-up too, her hair parted in a V at the top of her head, drawn down smoothly over her cheeks, and pinned back securely; her plain gown billowing from an already trim waistline.

Her eyes were gray-blue, her chin stood out firmly, and she had not lost her old habit of determination. Her sister Anna, dark-haired and pretty in an odd way, shut herself up in the parlor for hours at a time, and made up songs at the piano. She was determined to be a writer, and perhaps a musician as well. But Elizabeth couldn't make up her mind. There were so few things that a woman could do.

Teaching? She couldn't imagine herself being happy as a governess, shut up with some big family like a poor relative or half-servant. Although she helped with the teaching of her younger brothers and sisters in the schoolroom, since the family could no longer afford a governess, she often found herself impatient, and realized she had altogether too much energy for this kind of work.

Something hard, something that would take all of her
energies, something new that no other woman had ever done
—that was what she wanted. These were the secret thoughts
that she sometimes had as she sat with her sisters over the
endless family sewing, or listened to her little brother,
Howard, of whom she was especially fond, reciting his lessons.

The girls went right on studying, reading German and
French and history and even philosophy which Marion, who
was dreamy, seemed to understand best of all. But Elizabeth longed for something definite to do, something harder
and more important than helping with the housework and
the children, and assigning new lessons for herself to study.

"Whatever makes you so restless?" her mother complained.

Elizabeth went for long prowling walks by herself, came
home to scrub the floors in a flurry of housekeeping, and
then, tired and pale, seemed bored still with herself and
with all the rest of the world.

"I don't know what to do with myself!" This was her constant complaint.

And after a time, even the abolitionist meetings, which
she had attended at first so eagerly, ceased any longer to
interest her. Mr. Blackwell had also fallen away from his
first eager interest in the movement against slavery, because
of the mounting worries of his sugar business, which seemed
each year to do more poorly.

He came home worried, each night, and his health was
frail. The whole structure of his face, Elizabeth noticed, had
altered, and his skin was yellow after an attack of liver trouble which seemed to have become chronic.

In the next few years, the family moved frequently, always looking for a pleasanter but less expensive home.
Finally, in 1837, after the disastrous bank panic which had
destroyed what was left of Mr. Blackwell's failing business,
they took the longest move of all—across the mountains to
the city of Cincinnati, on the Ohio River.

They traveled by stagecoach and by canal boat, a long and a very fatiguing trip. And when the boat docked at the Cincinnati pier, Mr. Blackwell, who had sat shivering in a shawl most of the way, was taken ashore a very sick man.

What happened in the next few weeks was always painful for Elizabeth to remember. Before the household belongings could be unpacked, her father became very ill. A doctor was called and diagnosed the disease as biliary fever. There were purgings and cuppings and all sorts of medicines prescribed. But he did not get any better.

From the first, Elizabeth had known that her father would die. But when he was gone, she was stupefied, could hardly stir herself to help set the house to rights and consider what should be done about the family's acute financial condition.

There was very little money left. Elizabeth had a conference with her two older sisters. They were all grown women, Anna twenty-three, Marion two years younger, and Elizabeth now almost eighteen. Although all of them disliked teaching, they decided that the most practical thing to do would be to start a day-school for girls in their home.

Elizabeth went out canvassing for students, rang strange doorbells, presented her card, told of the expert teaching methods which her sisters employed. Much to her own surprise she found herself enjoying the challenge of this work. Like her father she had a talent for convincing people.

But the actual teaching she did not like, and so she let this part of the work fall more and more to her sisters and to her mother who found some relief from her grief in helping with the school.

In the crisis which had befallen them, all members of the family worked together courageously. Elizabeth's younger brother, Samuel, who at fifteen should have still been in school, came home, one day, to announce that he had called on a certain Major Gano at the court house and had been offered a post as a clerk. He began to work and was able soon after to find a place for his younger brother, Henry.

Several years passed. While the school was never prosperous, the family was able in one way or another to manage. The boys, who seemed to have a natural gift for business, became travelers for a hardware merchant of the city. They made long and successful trips by coach and by boat to sell the farm tools and household wares so much needed by the farmers of the surrounding country. And soon they were sending home fat envelopes to their mother and the problem of housekeeping at home was not now so difficult.

Elizabeth worked hard at the school, but was, as always, restless. With her mother and sisters she joined the church of Dr. W. H. Channing, a nephew of the famed Dr. Channing of Boston. Through this minister, who was a very well-educated man, the Blackwell girls became acquainted with an interesting family, the Beechers.

Dr. Lyman Beecher, a famous minister, had founded the Lane Theological Seminary. He had two daughters. One of them, Catherine, was a well-known writer of schoolbooks, and was the founder, as well, of one of the country's first schools for training women as teachers.

Her sister Harriet, who had married Dr. Calvin Stowe, one of the professors in the Lane Theological Seminary, was very interesting to Elizabeth. She was a writer, not famous, of course, because since she had married she had so little time for her work. Yet when she spoke about writing, Elizabeth felt that some day this pale, dark young woman would be famous, would do something important that the world wouldn't forget.

Elizabeth, who was lonely since the death of her father, liked to visit at the home of the Stowes. It was a household of crying children and untidy manuscripts lying on tables, on beds, on the floor. Yet Elizabeth felt at peace there. She would hold one of the babies and would listen with composure while Mrs. Stowe, her hair awry and her face smudged from cooking, read from one of her latest sketches, at the same time scolding the housemaid intermittently.

Sometimes there would be literary evenings in the home of the young Mrs. Stowe, and distinguished people of the city would attend. At one of these meetings, Elizabeth became acquainted for the first time with *The Dial* edited by a woman, Margaret Fuller, and with another magazine, *The Harbinger*, which proposed all sorts of reforms to make the American way of life better.

At these meetings, sometimes a gentleman would sit beside her, would ask permission to walk home with her after the session. But no one seemed to interest her. In her journal Elizabeth wrote, "I am amused, sometimes repelled." At the same time a feeling of want and loneliness filled her heart.

"What I need," she said over and over again to her sister Marion, "is some kind of absorbing occupation."

Marion could not understand her sister's restlessness. She, herself, was content to stay at home, help with the school, occasionally looking to the housekeeping of which Mrs. Blackwell had never been fond.

One evening, Elizabeth went with her sisters to attend a public debate in the Town Hall. The subject was women's rights. A fat and breathless gentleman said women's only career was to stay in the kitchen. A well-known attorney answered this argument sarcastically. Afterwards there was a great stir in the town about these issues. But it must be said for Elizabeth that she was not excited. Women's rights? In her home they had so long been taken for granted, that it seemed these gentlemen were debating a very old question indeed!

So the days passed, and Elizabeth, less and less interested in the school, was relieved, indeed, when her brothers, who were making good money now, insisted that it be given up.

"What in the world will I do with myself?" she said to her sister Marion, and envied the latter's contentment with household tasks and the endless reading in which she was absorbed.

But how could a person go on, taking in, taking in, and never *doing* anything with one's energy! She was twenty-three years old, and already the feeling was deepening in her that her life was being wasted.

The long, hot summer days seemed endless. She got up early, polished, cooked, dusted, going through the house like a whirlwind, and by mid-morning was on the porch, too impatient for sewing or reading.

"Something to do! Something to do!" she said, pounding her palm with her fist. She grew thin from her continued restlessness.

When she heard that a girls' district school in Kentucky needed a teacher, she decided to go, not because she liked teaching, but because it would be a change. Any kind of movement was better than this champing, futile energy that consumed her!

She traveled in a sheep boat along the Mississippi, and found her destination a village of dirty frame buildings on a desolate mud bank, with a tangle of Mississippi forest behind it. The people were sleepy, the manners of the town indolent, and the school not only had all of its windows broken, but was flooded with mud.

She scrubbed it herself, pasted up the windows, and on a Tuesday morning took her seat at the head of fourteen girls, all sleepy, all lazy, all very much disinterested in learning.

At the house where she boarded, there was no special room for the teacher. She was obliged to share her bedroom in the attic with three lanky, dull women, elder daughters of the household. Loving privacy intensely, she was never for one moment alone.

She had been lonely at home, here she was still lonelier. In spite of the fear of barking dogs and escaped slaves about whom she was forever being warned, she went for long walks in the woods alone. A young farmer, who had watched her several times, came up and asked bashfully if she would stroll with him, Elizabeth smiled, but refused him. She could not see herself as a farmer's wife.

When she came home in 1845, the family had moved to the pleasant suburb of Walnut Hills, where they occupied a house quite close to Lane Theological Seminary, and very near too to the residence of Professor Stowe and his writing wife, Mrs. Harriet Beecher Stowe, whom they were to see more and more frequently.

During the summer, Elizabeth studied music, translated German and French authors with her sister, Marion, and spent long hours wondering as before what, at the age of twenty-four, she was to do with her life.

An incident occurred at this time, which was upsetting to her, but which at the same time seemed to offer a suggestion. It was her habit to visit with a friend of her mother's, who was sick with a malignant disease and knew that she was dying.

Elizabeth would sit by the woman's bed, during the long, hot summer afternoons, and would read to her, or else they would talk together quietly.

"I have often wondered," said the sick woman, "why women, who are always preoccupied with the care of the sick, are not allowed to become physicians?"

Elizabeth looked at her. "If I could have been treated by a woman physician," said her friend, "perhaps my illness would have been better understood."

The next time Elizabeth came, the sick woman again spoke about this same subject. "Why don't you undertake the study of medicine?" she said.

Elizabeth, who was surprised at this odd proposal, replied almost indignantly that she hated everything connected with the body, and could not bear the sight of a medical book.

Then she remembered an incident which had occurred in her childhood. A new master who had been engaged to teach the children was very enthusiastic about the study of physiology, and one day brought into the schoolroom the eye of a bullock. Elizabeth had been repulsed at the sight of this object all bloody on its cushion of fat.

Elizabeth shuddered at the memory, and declared to her sick friend, "Study medicine? Why, that is the one subject that interests me least!"

"You object too strenuously," said the sick woman wisely.

And it was true. The suggestion fascinated Elizabeth, even though it also repelled her. No woman had ever been admitted to a medical school. In fact, as far as Elizabeth knew, and she began inquiring cautiously among her friends, no woman had ever made the attempt to gain admittance. She could not seem to dismiss from her mind the possibility of becoming a doctor. The very difficulties challenged her.

In her diary she wrote, "I must have something to engross my thoughts."

The death of her friend, a short time after their strange talk, caused her to think about the proposal even more seriously.

She began openly to discuss the project, first with the members of her family, and then with her friends. Dr. Reuben Mussey, family physician to the Blackwells, was horrified. No school in America would admit a woman. As for the French schools, which might be more liberal, how could he suggest that she go there?

"Why, the methods of instruction are such that no lady could stay there six weeks!" he exclaimed.

This opposition hardened Elizabeth. Here was something to sink her teeth into, to take hold of, to exert herself upon with utmost energy. Cautiously she spread the idea a little further, went to call one afternoon on her writing friend, busy Mrs. Harriet Beecher Stowe.

There was the usual turmoil in the house. The babies were crying underfoot, the maid had failed to follow some instructions, and Mrs. Stowe was frantically writing in the midst of the hubbub, on a corner of the dining-room table littered with some sewing she had abandoned, and at which the children were pulling constantly.

She called to the maid, scolded the children, and listened to Elizabeth, but only with half her thoughts. Her mind was on the half-written sheet under her hand.

"Study medicine!" she looked at Elizabeth uncomprehendingly, as though this suggestion on top of a crowded morning was almost more than her mind could take in. But when she saw that her friend was quite serious, she said she would talk the matter over with her husband, and would let her know in a few days what both of them thought. Her expression was not encouraging.

And indeed, her opinion, delivered the next day over a calm cup of tea, with babies and writing out of the way, was even less encouraging. It was an impossible undertaking, she said. Elizabeth would encounter insurmountable difficulties. Why didn't Elizabeth undertake something she could do at home, writing, for example. You could influence a great many people if you finally got the right subject. And she went on to talk of her own many unfinished writing projects.

Very much discouraged, Elizabeth said good-bye to Mrs. Stowe. Then, on a sudden impulse she went to call on a businessman of the town, shrewd, cool Mr. James H. Perkins, whom she had met once at a literary meeting. He received her in his counting house, getting off of his stool to take her hand and ask her to be seated. She told him she had come for advice.

"I have decided," she said, "to become a physician."

To her great surprise, he did not discourage her. "I do wish you would take the matter up, if you have the courage," he said. He looked at her thoughtfully. "And you have the courage, I know!"

Then he told her that he, himself, had once been interested in undertaking the study of medicine, but had been prevented from doing so. "I guess I didn't have the very quality that you possess, Miss Blackwell," he said.

Elizabeth went home excited. That night she took out her journal and words came almost spontaneously. "I hesitate as if I were about to take the veil," she wrote, and then with a stern expression on her lips she added, "but I am gradually coming up to the resolution."

She lay awake in the dark a long time, and in the morning wrote a letter to Dr. Abraham Cox, who had been their family physician in the East. She told him of her plans and inquired concerning the best medical schools in the country. She added that she would like his advice on the feasibility of a woman attending one of them.

When her brother Henry brought her the answer, one evening when he came home, her fingers trembled and she could hardly break the seal. But the communication was entirely cool. To be sure, it gave information as to schools, fees, and courses of study. But it carefully avoided the suggestion that she should try to enroll.

"I will not be dissuaded," cried Elizabeth, and having made the resolution she was beset at once with overwhelming problems. Where to go and how to get there? With whom to begin and what to do first? She had no money. A woman friend had in a moment of enthusiasm offered a loan of several thousand dollars. But by the time Elizabeth was ready to accept this help, by the time her mind was completely made up, her friend told her in the embarrassed way that people do when they go back on their promises, that all she could offer was a hundred dollars! Elizabeth thanked her and refused the loan.

But she was by no means discouraged. In her diary she wrote, that very evening, frowning as she put down the words, "I am more determined than ever to become a physician!"

She turned again to teaching, a work she disliked, but if she was to make the money for her education, it must be done quickly. She obtained a position in the South again, this time in a small school for girls run by a minister who had at one time been a physician. In corresponding with the Reverend John Dickson of Asheville, North Carolina, she told him of her desire to study medicine, and asked if he would be willing to give her some preliminary instruction in medical subjects.

It was agreed that he was to coach her in physics and chemistry, with some study perhaps of the theory of anatomy. In turn, she was to receive her room and board in the parsonage, and was to teach music and reading in the parsonage school. A small salary, which she could save, if she was careful, was also offered.

Elizabeth discussed the matter with her two brothers, Samuel and Henry. Both of them not only encouraged her, but insisted on making the eleven-day journey with her, by carriage along the Allegheny routes to North Carolina.

The trip along wild woods and steep mountain roads was exhausting, but the two young men, having deposited their sister safely, had to leave immediately for home. Elizabeth was very lonely as she stood at the parsonage window, on a rainy afternoon, her first in Asheville, and watched the carriage depart.

"We know," Henry had said as he left her, "how much you dislike teaching." And he had promised to help her. He was very proud of his sister's ambition.

"If my income increases," he said, "you won't have to be at this work long."

But the routine of teaching was not so dull for Elizabeth now, because as soon as the little girls were gone from the schoolroom, she shut herself up with the medical books that the Reverend Dickson had lent her, and studied so hard that this gentleman was amazed at her progress.

"If ever you get into a medical school," he said, "you will put the men students to shame!" He was a mild, quiet man, who himself had disliked the study of medicine, and he was surprised at her absorbed attention and very rapid progress.

But the other teachers at the school thought her ambitions peculiar, and did not hesitate, slyly, to say so.

One of them, a thin, sly young woman who had a sharp, witty way of belittling people, brought in a dead beetle one day and offered it "to the future Dr. Blackwell" as a subject for dissection.

Instead of becoming angry, Elizabeth took the dead insect, placed it on a shell that she kept on her desk, held it firmly with a hair pin, and then prepared to cut it open with her penknife. But when it came to actually touching the dead object on the shell, she hesitated.

Her friend laughed. "A fine doctor you would make!"

Elizabeth jabbed at the insect, holding her breath as she did it. A puff of yellow powder came out. There was nothing inside.

She laughed, and later wrote home, "It was my first exercise in dissection. I don't think I shall ever again be timid."

The next year she went to Charleston, where she obtained a position as teacher of music in a fashionable boarding school. In the evenings she studied medicine privately with Dr. Samuel H. Dickson, a relative of the Reverend Mr. Dickson, with whom she had first begun her studies.

Her new teacher was a well-known physician and also a professor in the medical school of the city. He was a large, well-built, friendly man, somewhat blunt in his manner, and impatient as a teacher.

She was cold with perspiration and very nervous at her first lesson. "I can promise you nothing," he said, "no recommendation, no assistance."

Moreover, he had given her to understand, quite plainly, that he doubted very much that any school would admit her. But if she wanted to study, he was not averse to giving her a few lessons.

In answer, Elizabeth opened her notebook. "Can we begin today?"

He gave her a look almost of admiration, and began at

once to tell her about the bony structure of the body, lecturing her on the great need for thoroughness in the study of anatomy.

"Where are the finest medical schools located?" Elizabeth asked him one day.

"Philadelphia, of course. It's the Paris of America, the medical capital of this country!" And he glanced at her as if wondering why she should ask such a question.

Elizabeth began to write letters at once to her friends, asking if they knew anyone at all in Philadelphia who might be able to help her.

She was recommended to Dr. Joseph Warrington, an elderly Quaker physician who was doing some very interesting work in regard to women. In his home he was training "gentlewomen" to become nurses, and for these women he had written a book of instructions on the care of the sick.

Elizabeth wrote to him confidently. Certainly such a man would understand her ambitions and would help her.

But his reply, while sincere, was disappointing. About her hope of studying medicine he wrote frankly, "I see many difficulties in the way of thy attainment," and with many quaint "thees" and "thous" and many religious expressions he tried to convince her that it would be much better if she were to devote herself to "the holy duties of nursing the sick."

"It is appropriate," he said, "that man be the physician and woman the nurse!"

Elizabeth folded the letter and put it into the book she had been reading. She closed the book vigorously, drew out a fresh sheet of paper, and biting her lip as she sometimes did when making up her mind suddenly on a difficult project, she sat down to reply to the Quaker physician.

She thanked him for his kind and thoughtful letter, and for his advice, which she would consider most carefully. Then she added, smiling, although the old determined look was on her face, that she looked forward with great anticipation to meeting him, since she was soon coming to Philadelphia, to seek entry into a medical school!

She went out at once to post the letter. And that night, lying in her bed, with her hands folded over her chest, she smiled again, and full of a feeling of strength and confidence, fell asleep. The decision was made.

CHAPTER THREE

AMONG THE PASSENGERS ON THE SAILING
packet from Charleston to Philadelphia, one May morning,
in 1847, was a young woman in a dove-colored gown, and a
white bonnet with very few ribbons or flowers upon it.

Her hair, the other women passengers had noticed, though
light in color and pleasant to look at, was not dressed in curls
or ringlets, as was the fashion, but was folded down neatly
on either side of her face. And throughout the entire passage,
instead of embroidering, or sewing on some little trifle, in her
chair on the deck, the young woman had kept to herself,
reading continuously from a heavy brown book.

Several young men on the boat had shown by their glances that they would be happy to tip their beavers to the studious young lady. But she did not look up. And as the towers and chimneys of Philadelphia came into view in the bright May morning light, she stood alone at the railing, and looked out on the approaching city.

With her hand shading her eyes, she tried to pick out what must be the white top of Jefferson Medical College, about which Dr. Dickson had told her. And where were the massed buildings of the University Medical School? To these two famous schools it was her intention to apply first. It had been arranged by her friends in Charleston that while she sought entry, she should have board, room, and private instruction in medicine from Dr. William Elder, a well-known physician and an author, too. He had written for many publications on reform, and was known as well for his liberal ideas on the education of women.

To the residence of Dr. Elder, on Seventh Street, Elizabeth now directed the cab. There she was greeted kindly by the doctor's lady, who preceded her up the stairs to a pleasant room at the front of the house, where a green lattice blind shut out the bright sunshine, and a deep curtained bed suggested to the traveler how tired she was.

Yes, she was tired. It was a fatigue Elizabeth felt more keenly, now that her journey was at an end. All winter she had been getting up at five in the morning to study Greek and anatomy, teaching eight hours a day in Mrs. Du Pre's school, where she was mistress of music, and then studying again in the evening over Dr. Dickson's lessons, until she fell asleep over the books.

Directly the school term was over, there had been a few dresses to prepare for her departure—she had gone all over the city seeking an inexpensive dressmaker—and many more hours of studying to do, before she could feel herself ready to come to Philadelphia to interview the doctors she must convince, if they were to help her in her desire to get into a medical school.

She had taken the packet to Philadelphia because this was the cheapest possible mode of travel. But she was a wretched sailor, and her studies aboard the ship had hardly been successful. Although the sea had been calm, the occasional dipping of the boat made her seasick, and her head had throbbed miserably all the way.

When her boxes, a large one of books and a small one of dresses, had been brought up to her room, she was half minded to take Mrs. Elder's advice and lie down on the curtained bed. The doctor was in the consultation room, his wife told her, and would not be free to see his student until after the midday meal.

But lying down in broad daylight seemed wasteful to Elizabeth. She thanked her hostess and said she preferred to unpack instead. Into the deep closet she hung her three summer gowns, and an all-purpose pelerine of sober black silk. The white bonnet, a gift from her mother, she laid on a paper and looked at it regretfully. One of darker hue would have been far less trouble. On the marble-topped table which she drew up to the window, she laid out her books.

At the midday dinner table, to which she went down somewhat diffidently, Dr. Elder spoke to her warmly, encouraging her efforts and advising her that she must at once begin some private instruction in anatomy. He had already made inquiry, he said, of a certain Dr. Joseph M. Allen, who operated a private school of dissection on College Avenue, near St. Stephen's Episcopal Church.

Of course, he said, slicing the roast and filling her plate abundantly, Dr. Allen's instruction could give her no medical credit. His was a purely tutorial school, attended by young men who needed brushing up in their studies at the medical colleges of the city.

Dr. Elder chuckled. "I may admit," he said, "that Dr. Allen's sensibilities were somewhat shocked at the notion of a student in petticoats!"

Elizabeth would have said something, but he interrupted her, cutting the food on his plate with precision and eating rapidly. "With a good grounding in chemistry, which I shall give you, and in anatomy, in which I hope Dr. Allen will instruct you, you will be better prepared than most men," he went on.

"You give me courage," said Elizabeth.

The doctor smiled. "From what my friend, Dr. Dickson, has written me, I would say, madam, that this is not a quality in which you are lacking, although you might as well lead a revolution as try to become a physician!"

He pushed his plate away, got up from the table unceremoniously. "The doctors are knocking their heads against each other for lack of business," he said. "One cups, the other blisters, the third gives calomel. Between them there are not enough patients to go around, nor enough new, fashionable and utterly notorious treatments with which to inveigle them. From their point of view the profession has small need of women physicians to add to their woes!"

Elizabeth liked the hearty, bluff remarks of this big, genial physician, and could not help smiling. They would get on, she knew, and already Philadelphia did not seem so strange to her, nor her task so hard.

The next day she paid a visit to the Philadelphia School of Anatomy, as Dr. Allen's dissection rooms were called. A quiet, gentle-speaking man, he received her in his study, a room at the front of the house which was permeated, every time the inner door was opened, with a thick sickening smell of disinfectants. This smell was to cling to Elizabeth for days, sticking in her throat and tincturing the food in her mouth so that she could scarcely swallow it.

The interview was over in a few minutes. Evidently prepared for his new student by Dr. Elder, the teacher of anatomy asked her only one question. "Madam," he said, putting the query directly, "are you prepared for these studies? Those who do not understand them, might call them unpleasant."

"I will not be troubled, I trust," said Elizabeth, quietly.

The doctor bowed. "Then come tomorrow at eight."

Before she went out, he asked her to stop for a moment and note down the supplies she must purchase. First he brought out a chest of instruments. "Four of these!" Then he held up a sharp, delicate knife. "Needles, forceps, scissors, a blow pipe, a single and a double hook . . ." He continued the list.

The purchase of the instruments caused her a little disquietude. The entry of a woman into a medical supply shop was enough of an event. But when instead of calling for a package for a brother or friend, this young woman asked to see a case of instruments and began to examine them, several students standing nearby moved up closer to stare.

As Elizabeth made her choice, one of them came up beside her. "Perhaps," he said, and his voice was not polite, "madam fancies herself a doctor?"

Elizabeth looked at him. "Not yet," she said, and left the shop, carrying her package tightly. It was very precious to her.

From Mrs. Elder's maid she borrowed an enormous apron which had to be tied twice round her waist. Then in the evening she carefully ripped out the deep cuff from her gray muslin gown, so that the full sleeve could be drawn away from the wrist, pinned close and snug to the arm while working.

At a quarter to eight the next morning she was in Dr. Allen's dissection room. There were no other students present.

"They come later in the day," explained the doctor.

"Take a seat on the stool, madam," he went on, and took his place at a long wooden table by the window, under which hung a bucket of disinfectant.

"This," he said, "is the dissection table. The lesson today is on the structure and construction of the wrist. As I name these parts, in the specimen on the table, you will note and describe them in your copybook."

On the table lay a human arm, severed at the shoulder. Yellow and lifeless, soggy from soaking in disinfectant, it was a repulsive object to behold.

Elizabeth felt dizzy, and her color must have changed, because the doctor looked at her sternly as he fingered his dissection instruments. Then without speaking he began to work.

She watched him as he inserted the knife, and with swift, deft movements, opened the skin, and layer by layer began exposing muscles, nerves, and tendons. As he named each part and described it, she bent forward to look, and wrote down what she had seen.

She became so absorbed that she forgot her repugnance. In fact, as he uncovered sheath after sheath of silvery fascia and intricately laced muscle, a kind of fascination took hold of her and when he put down the knife, at last, she spoke out almost involuntarily. "What a beautiful construction," she said, speaking almost with a sigh, and indeed she was deeply moved. "It fills one with reverence."

Doctor Allen, washing his hands in a basin behind the door, glanced back at her. "You have learned more than most students," he said.

She felt her cheeks glowing, and taking her apron off, hung it on the hook he had pointed out to her.

The next day, with men students at work nearby, she continued the dissection of the wrist, looking from time to time in her textbook which she had placed on the window. The men, after their first silent shock of surprise, got used to the notion of a woman in the dissection room, and treated her as she wished to be treated, with utter indifference. Dr. Allen encouraged her work, but said it was hardly likely that she could gain entry into a medical school, "which is indeed a pity, madam," he added.

Elizabeth went calmly on. She went to see Dr. Samuel Jackson, famous chairman of the Institutes at the University, and one of the oldest professors in Philadelphia.

She found him, one evening, in the study of his roomy, imposing home on Seventh Street, a small bright-faced, gray-haired man, who looked up from his newspaper and spoke to her abruptly but in a not unfriendly way.

"Well, what is it? What do you want?" he asked.

These questions, Elizabeth knew, were quite unnecessary. He had already had a letter from Dr. Elder, and another from Dr. Dickson, and Elizabeth knew he was well aware of the nature of her visit. But she was not resentful. She was pleased that he did not get up from his chair. He was receiving her as a student.

"I want to study medicine," she said. "I want to become a physician."

The doctor put down his paper. "There has never been a woman student in our school," he said, "nor at any other institution of medical instruction in the States. In fact," he went on, "I know of no country, madam, in which such a request has been made—or granted."

He spoke with patience as though explaining an entirely impossible matter to a stubborn and persistent child.

Elizabeth leaned forward. "I am quite aware . . ." she began, but he continued speaking as though he had not heard her.

"The gentlemen in our classes," he went on, still speaking patiently, and with the air that she had proposed something quite fantastic, "would find it disquieting to have a member of the other sex present in their midst!"

At this Elizabeth felt forced to protest. "What I request," she said, and despite a sincere effort at self-control, her voice became heated, "is, believe me, neither improper nor immodest. Women were the first physicians, I have heard, and I see no cause for keeping them from a study for which, by nature, they are so well fitted. Do we not tend the sick, in our homes, and care for the children . . ."

At this point the doctor interrupted her. "Indeed!" said the little gray-haired physician, "and if your ambition is to serve those who are helpless, then the holy profession of nursing is open, and should, madam, engage your fullest zeal!"

"Not that!" cried Elizabeth. "I want to become a physician, to learn the ills of the body and to attend to women who need me!"

She thought of her mother's sick friend, and how the proposal of studying medicine had come from her. With sudden impulse, she told the doctor the story.

He listened attentively, from time to time passing his hand over his chin. Elizabeth felt sure that the expression on his face changed.

When she had finished, the little doctor cleared his throat. "The barriers," he said, "may not be insurmountable!"

Elizabeth felt her heart jump, then the sudden weakness of elation. "When shall I come back?" There was hope in the question.

"I shall confer with my colleagues," the doctor promised. On Monday, he might have an answer to give her.

She walked fast in her long skirts, and at the turn of the street, felt almost like running, she was so eager to get back to Dr. Elder's study to tell him the news.

Elizabeth studied so fervently that night and the next, that in a few days she covered more ground than in weeks of her ordinary plodding. At the table Mrs. Elder remarked the her guest must for certainty have been pinching her cheeks, they were indeed so vivid. She ate with good appetite; all her food tasted delicious; she heard herself laughing; and was surprised at her own happiness.

But on Monday, facing Dr. Jackson with exuberance, she received like a fall of cold water the crushing answer.

He had spoken to his fellow professors, he said, and all were opposed.

"I regret, madam," he concluded, and Elizabeth could see from his expression that he really was sorry, "my inability to help you."

She pressed her lips together. "I shall try the other schools nonetheless, Dr. Jackson," she said. He shook her hand, but did not encourage her.

She left the house slowly. There seemed no strength in her body. How hot and dusty the city had grown! She walked past a bustle of carriages, her head down, her hands hanging limp at her sides, then with sudden purpose, crossed the way and turned toward tree-shaded Chestnut Street. She would visit Dr. William Edmonds Horner!

The brilliant dean of the University School of Medicine had told Dr. Jackson emphatically that he could not look with favor upon the entry of a woman to the course of medical studies. Very well, he was the very man to see. She mounted the steps, rang the bell emphatically and asked the maid to announce her.

Dr. Horner was a small man with frail shoulders and a body deformed by illness, but his expression was sharp and keen. He listened intently while she spoke, but his expression was inscrutable.

"I cannot help you, madam," he said, when Elizabeth had finished, "much as I respect your high resolve in wishing to give yourself to our difficult profession."

She wondered if there was an edge of sarcasm in this remark, and with this thought a flush of anger came to her face. The feeling of discouragement and weakness left her, and she felt determined and strong.

With an enthusiasm which was half anger, she laid before Dr. Horner the same arguments which had appealed to his friend, Dr. Jackson. And as he listened, his expression seemed to change, became almost friendly.

Finally he rose. "Even if I were in favor, Miss Blackwell,"

he said, "I would not feel it my duty to overcome the disinclination of my fellow professors."

As she thanked him for the interview, he seemed to relent. At the door he made the suggestion that she might try the new Homeopathic Medical College on Filbert Street. She might also, he said, go to see Dr. J. B. Biddle, director of Franklin College.

"What we cannot do, being one of the greatest schools in America, these lesser institutions might undertake with impunity." And quietly he closed the door after her.

Elizabeth sighed, felt a sudden flood of depression. Although Dr. Horner meant to be kind, he was telling her quite clearly that no medical school of good standing would ever receive her.

In her room, where the warmth of the day lingered even after it grew dark, she changed to a muslin gown, bathed her face, holding the cold cloth to her forehead, and sat down to study. But the heat from the lamp gave her a headache, and the anatomy she was memorizing wheeled in her head. Turning down the student lamp, she laid her cheek on the window sill. The trees were heavy in the darkness and from the street below came the sound of footsteps, and voices.

"What is it for?" she said. "Why am I struggling?"

And for an instant her life again felt without purpose and wasted. She reached for the bed in the darkness and fell asleep.

In the morning, she visited another professor of the University faculty. "I shall see them all before I give up," she told Dr. Elder, and he had encouraged her.

But on the way to Seventh Street, in the bright, hot fatiguing June sunshine, her depression almost overwhelmed her. The medical schools would not have her. Private study, excellent as it might be, would not gain her a medical degree. Besides, with museums, hospital wards, libraries

and all similar aids closed to her, how far could she go even in private studies?

To Dr. William Darrach, a tight-lipped gentleman with a high forehead and cold eyes, she forced herself to speak persuasively.

"The subject is a novel one, madam," he said at last. "I have nothing to say either for or against it."

Elizabeth looked surprised. "But, sir!"

"You have awakened trains of thought upon which my mind is taking action," he said coldly, "but I cannot express my opinion to you either one way or another."

Elizabeth leaned forward anxiously, looking at Dr. Darrach directly. "Your opinion, I fear, is unfavorable?"

The doctor seemed annoyed at being pressed to commit himself. "I beg you, madam," he said, speaking slowly and with more than necessary distinctness, "to understand that I express no opinion one way or another. The way in which my mind acts in this matter I do not feel at liberty to unfold."

Elizabeth got up and asked dispiritedly if she might call on the other professors at the college.

"I cannot take the responsibility of advising you," was the curt reply.

Elizabeth reached for the door handle, then turned toward him desperately. "Can you not grant me admittance to your lectures? May I not believe that you do not feel unfavorable to my scheme?"

At this remark, Professor Darrach, quite out of patience, turned to her with anger. "You may believe no such thing," he admonished, "and I beg leave to state clearly," he repeated, "that the operation of my mind in regard to this matter I do not feel at liberty to unfold."

In her diary, after telling briefly about this fruitless visit, Elizabeth wrote down an unhappy comment that night. "So I got up in despair, leaving Dr. Darrach's mind to take action on the subject at his leisure."

From the doctor's study she had gone stubbornly to the anatomy room on College Avenue, where she had spent the whole afternoon working doggedly on a particularly hard assignment. Dr. Allen stopping at her table to watch her work made an approving comment. But she was too discouraged to take any pleasure in his remark.

That evening, Dr. Elder called her into his consultation room. A thin, pale servant girl, who had come in with a cough, was awaiting diagnosis. With Elizabeth beside him, the doctor told the girl to bare her shoulders. Then, laying Elizabeth's palm to the moist skin, he instructed her to tap, listening for the sounds of congestion in the lung. Then he gave Elizabeth the stethoscope, and as she listened through it for the first time, she identified a surge that reached her ears like the swell of distant waters. It was the sound of the heart!

Elizabeth was fascinated. If Dr. Elder had permitted it, she would have stayed on and on, there in the consulting room. It was an epochal moment in her life. Now she knew beyond all shadow of a doubt that in spite of all her discouragements, she meant to be a physician.

She went to call on Dr. Warrington, the kind old Quaker physician to whom she had written in such confidence that she was coming to Philadelphia "to enroll in a medical school."

He listened to the story of her trials without speaking. Then softly, like a father giving unhappy directions to a child, he said, "Elizabeth, it is of no use. Thee cannot gain admission to these schools."

When she persisted, saying desperately that she must get into a school, would go to any length to do so, he made a suggestion that astonished her. "Then thee must go to Paris and don masculine attire to gain the necessary knowledge!"

"But I want to go as a woman!" It was almost a cry, and

she left him hurriedly. But back she came the next day to talk more calmly.

Dr. Joseph Pancoast, the professor of surgery at Jefferson Medical College, whom she had visited in the meantime had astounded her by making the same suggestion.

"But that's impossible for me," said Elizabeth. "I can't masquerade. I must be accepted as I am and for what I am. Otherwise what good will I do for the women who are to follow?"

Some of the arguments she heard against admitting women to medical practice were so trifling and small that she hardly could answer them. That men would be jealous of women, afraid of their competition and cleverness had never even occurred to her. Yet this notion was put to her bluntly one day by the dean of one of the smaller and less reputable schools to which she had been driven in despair.

"You cannot expect us to furnish you with a stick to break our heads with," he said crudely, and went on to tell her how hard it was for physicians to make a living. "Now that every greengrocer's son fancies himself a medical student," he said, "there will soon be more doctors than patients. As for women, with their wiles and connivances, their parties and their clever social ways, why in no time at all, they would be taking all our patients away from us!"

Elizabeth listened with amazement. The school was shabby, in an unpainted building. Yet even this embittered and disgruntled professor would not have her as a student there, saying that a small and struggling school could not risk the scandal of permitting a female student in the lecture room.

In desperation she returned to Dr. Warrington, who again suggested that if she wanted to study she must go to Paris.

"I shrink extremely from the idea of giving up the attempt in America and going to France," she wrote in her journal.

Yet at Dr. Warrington's suggestion she went to call on Dr. William Ashmead of the Philadelphia Lying-in-Charity Hospital, who had studied in France himself, and might advise her on a course of action.

He was most disapproving of her entire plan. "I most earnestly advise you, madam," he said, "to give up these unnatural ambitions, and devote yourself to pursuits more in keeping with the true aptitudes of your sex!"

Elizabeth went away angry. "I am more impelled now than ever," she reported to Dr. Warrington, whom she now saw frequently. "Dr. Ashmead gave me not one sensible argument!"

He glanced at Elizabeth, half-smiling. "That was a visit," he said, "that I would have spared thee, but thee would not permit it."

In her room that evening she worked late, not turning down the lamp until it was almost dawn. When she went out to post the letters she had written, it was almost with a feeling of hopelessness that she let them slip from her hand. To the College of Physicians and Surgeons in New York, and to the University of New York City, she had addressed herself earlier, when it was quite clear that no Philadelphia school would receive her. Both had sent courteous refusals. She began now to write in turn to the smaller, so-called "country schools" of medicine.

From Harvard, Bowdoin and Yale, she had already had refusals. Now came answers from Woodstock College, from a small school near Albany, New York, and from another institution in Vermont.

"It may well be," Dr. Elder advised, "that one of these smaller schools, wishing to draw public attention to its existence, might do so by admitting a woman."

Elizabeth was too tired and too despondent to take issue with this kind of reasoning.

The hot days of July had lengthened into the breathless afternoons of August, with not a leaf stirring on the trees. All the professors had gone out of the city to their country homes or to nearby watering places. There was no one left to see in Philadelphia. The dissection room, under the eaves of the wooden frame structure on College Street, was hot and odorous. Most of the students were gone, and Dr. Allen, seeing Elizabeth there, one afternoon, white and tired over the instruments she was polishing, advised her that he would close the school for the duration of the hot weather.

Her mother had written that her sisters, Anna, Marion, Emily, and Sarah Ellen, were at the seashore. Although Henry and Samuel were remaining at the Walnut Hills house, engaged with their new hardware business and so not able to join them. George, out of school for the summer, would spend his holidays with the family. Would she not come also? The briefest visit from her missing daughter would please her.

Elizabeth went, glad to get away from the city heat and the hourly tension of waiting, but unhappy that she had no news to bring home.

The cottage, an old yellow frame house, about a quarter of a mile inland from the sea, had occupants in every room, books thrown about, and the usual talk of writing, reading and intellectual projects of every kind. Her sister Anna had borrowed a shabby pianoforte and was busy in the parlor at the front of the house, where she shut herself up each morning to work on a group of songs she was expecting shortly to publish.

Marion, still suffering from headaches and lassitude, looked to the housekeeping, and on the days when she felt better, read the heavy philosophy books which no one else in the family could understand.

Emily was tired of teaching, and very restless. Sarah Ellen wanted to be a writer, and locked herself up at the top of the house, where Mrs. Blackwell said if the heat could set the pot simmering, then Sarah Ellen must indeed bring forth a work of genius.

All the Blackwell girls, like Elizabeth, had proven indifferent to suitors, although Anna, more fervent than the others, had once had a romance, a secret romance, which echoed turbulently in her poems, the very same poems that the dark-haired, intense poet and critic, Edgar Allan Poe, had praised so highly.

But as for attracting husbands, these unusual young women were altogether too frank and too casual with men to entice them. It was part of their belief in equality to treat men like equals and expect to be treated like equals themselves.

As for romance, the very breath of it seemed to make them cooler, more comradely.

"I guess," said Elizabeth, "that we're just not the marrying kind!"

To this remark, Henry, if he had been there, would have taken vigorous exception. "You mean there are just no men fine enough to appreciate women of your kind," he had once declared.

And in this favorite remark of his there was probably some truth. Where were there, in this day, men like the Blackwells, who had the courage to accept women as equals?

Because Elizabeth had not been home for a long time, there was a great deal of Cincinnati news to be reported upon. She sat on a wobbly ottoman listening to her mother when the others had gone, and asked many eager and interested questions.

Henry, who had been traveling on horseback through the wild country of Wisconsin, Minnesota, and Iowa, to take orders for hardware, had done so well, her mother told her, that he was now about to be made a partner in the business.

Several times, on visits home, he had spoken at abolitionist meetings, and like his father, the elder son had written verses against slavery. Several of his poems had been read aloud before the anti-slave society of Cincinnati, and several had been published in the papers.

Their friend, the Reverend Lyman Beecher, her mother reported, was still guiding the destinies of Lane Theological Seminary, where Dr. Stowe still remained as professor of Biblical literature. His wife, the ambitious Harriet, was said to be writing a book.

A visitor to the Stowe's, Elizabeth's mother went on to tell her, had given a very inspiring oration on the subject of women's rights. Her name was Lucy Stone, she was a schoolteacher from Massachusetts, who lectured for the abolitionists sometimes, and she spoke "most forthrightly and courageously."

"Henry would court her," confided her mother, "if she would let him. He tells me that in firmness of character she resembles you more than any other person he has known!"

Elizabeth wondered how firm her own character might be, and told of her difficulties during the past few months in Philadelphia.

Emily, who had returned earlier than the others, listened thoughtfully. "I too would like to undertake the study of medicine," she said.

Elizabeth looked at her ruefully. "Wait until I have done better than bump my head." She told her mother that if she could not get training in the States, it was her intention to go to Europe. Even in this expensive project Henry had promised to help her. There was no end to his ardor for her plans.

In the evening, Elizabeth spoke with her sister Anna about the plan for European medical study. Anna told her that she might not be alone if she went.

"I have been planning to go myself," she said, adding that several of the papers to which she contributed had encouraged her in her plan of becoming a "lady correspondent," for their foreign news columns.

"The Lord help you with all your ambitions," said Mrs. Blackwell, and went into the house.

Sitting in the dark, with the scent of lilacs around them, and the sea mist hanging from the trees, the girls talked of their plans. Only Marion was silent.

Elizabeth put her hand in her elder sister's lap. "You are the most gifted of all, Marion. I don't know what impels the rest of us to so much doing . . ."

Six weeks later she went back to Philadelphia. It was cool in the city. Rainy days came. The leaves fell from the trees. And then the sun came out, bringing a period of breathtaking Indian summer. The autumn sunshine was good, and Elizabeth felt languid in her room. The winter sessions at the schools of medicine would start now in less than two weeks.

From several of the smaller schools to which she had written early that summer, there were still no answers. Then one day, three letters came. All said no. Only one inquiry still remained unanswered. Only one school, a small unimportant school, tucked away in the upper reaches of New York State, almost near the borders of Canada, was left to be heard from. It was the Geneva Medical College, located in the town of Geneva, at the head of one of the long "Finger Lakes," an obscure and little-heard-of school.

For this reply Elizabeth waited, but almost without hope. Only a feeling of stubbornness held her up. It was impossible for her to give in.

On the twenty-seventh of October the letter came. She bit her lip as she took it, then waited for the maid to go down so that she could open it alone.

There were two pages inside, one a letter, the other some kind of official document. The writing swam together under her eyes. Her hands were trembling, her body felt numb. She could scarcely make out what she was reading. "Instructed by the faculty . . . a quorum of the faculty. . . . I send you the results of their deliberations . . ."

And on the sheet enclosed she read, couched in formal language, the reasons for her acceptance. "Resolved that one of the radical principles of a Republican Government is the universal education of both sexes; that to every branch of scientific education the door should be open equally to all; that the application of Elizabeth Blackwell to become a member of our class meets with our entire approbation."

On November fourth, Elizabeth left Philadelphia, traveling all night to reach Geneva College where the winter lectures on medicine had already begun. She would be two weeks late for the opening sessions.

In her reticule, held closely in her hand, was a precious document, the letter of acceptance which she had copied out on parchment for safekeeping!

CHAPTER FOUR

I RUN A CORRECT HOUSE, A VERY CORRECT house," said the landlady, and would have shut the door, except that Elizabeth put out her hand, and without invitation stepped over the doorsill.

"Please, Miss Waller," she said. "It's because of the fine reputation of your boarding house that I've come to you . . ." And motioning to the cabman to unload her boxes, she followed the prim Scotswoman into the house.

The house smelled pleasantly of wax and of polish, and the fluted curtains stiff with starch hung in exact folds over the windows. Elizabeth sat down on a stiff chair, and drawing off her gloves as though she had been asked to make herself at home, began to speak rapidly, but in a soft, gentle and persuasive voice.

"I must live near the college," she said, "and I assure you that my conduct, no matter what your views on female education may be, will be blameless! I have the highest recommendations . . ."

The Scotswoman shook her head.

But Elizabeth resolutely opened her black satin reticule and drew out the letters of recommendation with which she had furnished herself.

She had called at every other boarding place in the village, and had everywhere else been refused. What an excitement there had been in the town as soon as it was known that a woman had come to the college to study!

The greatest indignation and curiosity had been aroused. At the inn, where she had been staying for the first few days, the other women guests drew away their skirts as she passed, and little boys followed her in the street shouting an improvised rhyme. "Doctor! Doctor in petticoats. Do you cure corns? Or do you cure colds?"

"You must take me, Miss Waller," she said. "You are a kind and a decent woman, I can see."

"It will ruin my house!" said Miss Waller.

Elizabeth looked at her. "I do not believe, madam," she said, "that you would care overly much what people might think!"

There was a tremor at the corner of the prim lips.

"And I do not believe, madam," said Elizabeth, throwing herself entirely on the other woman's mercy, "that you would consult anything but your own conscience."

The landlady smiled. "You are a shrewd judge of character," she said.

Elizabeth got up triumphantly and opening the door, she called to the cabman. "Where," she said to Miss Waller, "shall I tell him to put my boxes?"

"Mind you," said the landlady, holding out her skirts before her as she began to mount the stairs, "the room is small, the stairs are steep." She stopped on the first landing to catch her breath. "And I cannot account to you for the civility of my guests!"

Elizabeth climbed breathlessly behind her. "I shall not contaminate them."

As she was coming down the stairs to supper that night, her first meal in the house, she overheard a remark from the dining room that brought a hot stinging rush of blood to her cheeks.

It was a woman's voice, high, dry and malicious. "Brazen I call it, and utterly shameless!"

There was a murmur and then the indignant voice again. "Does she wear trousers, I pray, and smoke black cigars?"

"But Amelia," it was the softer voice, rather plaintively, "certainly we should speak to her, if we're to sit at the same table!"

Elizabeth who couldn't bear to listen another instant longer, lifted the *portière* and entered the dining room.

Immediately there was a frozen silence. "Good evening," she said politely.

The guests looked down into their soup. There were four of them, two maiden ladies, one timid and pale with a waterfall of false curls put on slightly crooked, and the other a big woman with bony features and sharp eyes, who looked at Elizabeth disapprovingly, then at once addressed herself to her dinner.

A young woman with a high nose and dark hair sat beside a dull-looking young man with carefully turned whiskers. These, Elizabeth decided, must be the bridal pair whom Miss Waller had mentioned, a young doctor and his wife, who were newly come to the village and were looking for a suitable location.

She addressed a remark to the lady about the weather, and was pointedly ignored. Miss Waller, who had taken her place at the table, rather late, pursed her lips and glanced at Elizabeth with a look that seemed to say, "I warned you. This is all you can expect," and at once the landlady began to speak about the high prices of food and the difficulties of getting good boarding places. It was almost like a warning to her guests to behave themselves.

In her room that evening, Elizabeth wrote a letter to her sister Marion, describing what had happened in the town and at the boarding house.

"I had evidently so shocked Geneva propriety," she said, "that the theory was established at once that either I was a bad woman, whose designs would gradually become evident, or that, being insane, an outbreak of insanity would soon be apparent."

The strange reception she had gotten at the school had puzzled and depressed her too. In spite of the beautiful letter of acceptance which the college had sent her, she was made to feel that she wasn't welcome and that her presence was an embarrassment to the faculty. In fact, the registrar, a gentleman with lank sideburns and an apprehensive air, conveyed to her quite clearly the notion that she had shown a great breach of good taste in presenting herself.

This was very disappointing to Elizabeth who didn't know and was not for a long time to find out that her acceptance was entirely the result of a joke and an accident!

What had happened was that the faculty of Geneva College had decided, of course, that they could not admit a woman. But since the college was small and needed funds badly, and Elizabeth's request had been accompanied by an urgent note from Dr. Elder, who was known as an influential physician, they found it a little embarrassing to refuse the request.

It was suave Dr. Charles A. Lee, the dean of the college, who hit on a decorous solution. The faculty would not refuse, but what if the student body objected! Then a polite

but regretful note could be written to the important Philadelphia physician. "The faculty is liberal. We are willing.
But what can we do, if our students refuse!"

Accordingly it was decided that the matter should rest
with the student body which could be depended upon
to refuse admission to a young woman. And to make doubly
certain it was provided that in deciding on Miss Blackwell's
petition the vote of the Student Council of Geneva College,
must be unanimous! Never in the history of the school had
there been a unanimous vote on any measure, no matter how
trivial. So the young woman was as good as rejected already.

"Which is a pity!" round, jolly Dr. James Webster had
said. He was the anatomy professor, who was never too
dignified for a joke. "If we admitted her, it might cause
some notoriety. And even that is better than not being
heard of at all."

As usual, this indecorous remark was frowned down.

What the dean and the faculty members had not counted
upon was the mood of the students, who happened at this
time of the year to be particularly restless.

The school term had opened during a spell of dismal, late
autumn rains. And then suddenly, as happens in the northern towns near the borders of Canada, came a period of
breathless, beautiful Indian summer. Windows were thrown
open. The lake, visible from the classrooms of the college,
became blue as sapphire under a hot, almost mid-summer
sun. The blanched grass gave out a sweet fragrance and
insects hummed dreamily.

The soothing sound, the sweet smell, the warmth, flowed
into the lecture room. A languor came over the class followed by a strange rising restlessness. The students, most
of them country boys, used to heavy farm work, loud
sudden shouts of laughter, and rough-and-tumble games
and pranks, had not yet accustomed themselves to the
decorum of the classroom.

Under the quiet in the amphitheatre that morning, when

the dean appeared to read his announcement, there was a hidden excitement which expressed itself in darts of paper sent sailing through the air, mysterious notes passed from hand to hand, and a foot put out here and there to make a student stumble and the whole classroom roar.

The dean read his message, the letter from Miss Blackwell, the note from Dr. Elder, the faculty's recommendations.

A lady asking to be admitted to the class! How hilarious! There were shouts of "hear! hear!" and an uproarious stamping of feet.

All during the hot, late autumn afternoon the whispered hilarity and excitement continued. And that evening, for the first time in the history of the school, not a single student was missing from the students' meeting.

Everyone was in the mood for hilarity, pranks, and excitement. The young men leaped on chairs, and with mock gestures and exaggerated, grandiloquent phrases made long and bellicose speeches. "Down with the men! Hear! Hear! Hurrah for the women, God bless them!" And there was such a thumping and a roaring and a shouting on every side that the chairman, knocking for quiet for a full half hour, gave up finally in vain, and with a gesture of resignation threw the meeting open to all who wished to express themselves.

There was no lack of volunteers. Every moment a new speaker got up, shouted louder, declaimed more hysterically. And the more extravagantly the orators spoke, the more they were cheered.

"Bravo! On with the ladies. . . . We vote for trousers for all!" someone screamed.

"Quiet!" shouted the chairman. "All in favor of admitting Elizabeth Blackwell . . ."

There was a hilarious shout of "yea!" Only one timid voice from a corner was heard in a trebly "No!"

"What? He opposes us?" Instantly a rush was made for

the corner of the room from which this opposing sound had come. The frightened voter, passing under boisterous feet and fists, was finally picked up with the wind quite knocked out of him. Shoved onto the platform, and with some encouragement from a fellow student who held him by the back of the neck while another pummeled him, he sputtered out the final "yea" which made the vote unanimous!

Afterwards some of the cooler heads regretted what had happened. Admit a woman! The college had made itself ridiculous. But there was nothing to do but draw up a letter of welcome which the members of the class somewhat ruefully signed.

And the dean, who had his misgivings, could not keep from expressing them in the note that he enclosed to Miss Blackwell.

"There are no fears," he wrote, "but that you can, by judicious management, not only disarm criticism, but elevate yourself without detracting in the least from the dignity of the profession."

But of Miss Blackwell's undertaking, it was, he admitted, one which "some may deem bold in the present state of society." And he sent the letter off hoping that the young woman would after all lose her courage and would, for the good of the school, fail to appear.

So when Elizabeth arrived, two weeks after the autumn sessions had begun, and when the whole faculty and the student body had begun to look on her acceptance as only a bad dream, a kind of accident which everyone wanted to forget, no one, either students or faculty, knew just what to do with her!

For Elizabeth the first three days were bewildering. She had no books, didn't know where to get any, went from professor to professor, opened one door after another, was confused with running about the great college building— and had continually the feeling that she was not wanted, that she constituted an embarrassment to everybody, an embarrassment they were too polite to express, but which they couldn't after all conceal.

The groups of students, standing in the hall between class periods, froze when she approached and seemed almost to draw away as she passed. The professors too were so distant, that even if she had burst out shouting, it seemed to her they would not have understood what she was saying, and could not have helped her.

Her affairs, after three days of running about, were still unsettled. The anatomy professor was away, and in his absence the demonstrator refused to admit her to the anatomy class.

Elizabeth, who was very tired, could not help showing her temper. "I worked under Dr. Allen in Philadelphia," she said with warmth. "I am a registered student in this school."

"That," said the demonstrator, "is not my fault, madam!"

She spent a gloomy evening in her room that night, nursing the smoky "airtight" which gave out more fumes than heat, and fretting. No books to study, no lessons to prepare, and three weeks of the racing term were gone already. Would they never let her get started? In four months the year's work would be over, and how could she possibly make up all that she had missed?

She paced the floor until a knocking from the room below announced that the maiden lady ensconced in the chamber beneath her was annoyed at her footsteps.

"Well," said Elizabeth hotly to herself, "it's good to be noticed to that degree!"

She would have gone for a walk through the town, but her coming had awakened such a curiosity, that after one or two trips she hadn't the courage to go out again. The evening before, she had gone down to the general store, at the foot of the hill, to buy a handful of raisins and almonds to munch in her room. But on the way there, and during her return, there had been such gapings and gaspings, such inarticulate stares and such a whispering behind her as she passed, that she was glad to climb the hill to the college and to her room in a hurry, arriving breathless and flushed, and ready for tears—for her a very unusual condition.

"I will demand my rights!" she said, speaking to herself. And drawing down the counterpane of her bed preparatory to retiring, she gave the pillows a thunderous whack.

Then—"That's for you, Miss Prim," she said, as she let her boots drop noisily to the floor.

The next morning she went to school, along the short path over the brim of the hill, in a belligerent mood. Even the beauty of the lake, dark and ruffled under the rain, did not stir her, and she arrived ready almost for a hot declaration of her rights.

But surprisingly enough, she was told that the dean, Dr. James Hadley, wanted to see her. And as if he had had a change of heart, Dr. Hadley smiled at her nervously, then said he himself would conduct her to her first class.

While Elizabeth waited in an anteroom, he went into the amphitheatre and made what sounded like a long speech. Elizabeth could hear his voice and thought she could hear also the palpable silence that greeted it.

Then he put out his head, beckoned, and opening the door before her with exaggerated courtesy, he bade her enter the room. In spite of his dignified manner, there was a tense and agitated quality in his voice, as he announced, "Miss Blackwell, our new student."

The class greeted Elizabeth in silence. The rows of young men, sitting in tier on tier round the sides of the steep-sloping amphitheatre, seemed to swim before her eyes. But she managed to smile, nod her head, and taking the seat that was pointed out to her near the lecturer's platform, she removed her bonnet, and although her heart was thudding in her ears, her fingers were trembling, she laid out her stock of pencils, neatly sharpened beforehand, and opened her notebook.

And after a time she forgot the room, the silent young
men above and around her, the stares, the neck cranings,
the faint whisperings, and writing rapidly, listened only to
the lecturer.

She hastened unafraid to the other classes, sat transported through six hours of classwork and lectures. The
dissection period came in the evening, the students beginning at eight and working until almost midnight. Anatomy,
physiology, chemistry, pharmacy, therapeutics: there was
so much to learn, so much! Could one person in one lifetime
encompass it all, master this wide and profound knowledge?

How intricate the human body was, how wonderful!
Filling one with awe, and yes, with despair too. How
could any one single human being ever learn all of its
secrets?

At the supper table that evening she ate without looking
up, hardly noticing who else was present, what they said,
or how they looked at her; if they noticed her at all!

When the meal was over, she took up her books, repaired
at once to the school, and once more to the dissection room.
But again she found that the professor of anatomy was not
yet returned, that the demonstrator still would not admit
her.

The next morning, however, the professor returned. What
a round, jolly, friendly little person he was! The meeting
took place in the dean's office, to which she had been sum-
moned, and instantly she liked the knobby-nosed little
professor with his chubby cheeks, round belly, and twinkling
eyes which surveyed her with such a contagious merriment
that even the dean was affected by it.

The little doctor put out his hand, took Elizabeth's. "So
this is the daring young woman!" he said. "Capital! Your
plan is capital!"

He bent his head slyly, folded his hands over his stomach,
looked at her from under a merry eyebrow, then asked as

if in a more serious afterthought, the fields in which she had already had preparation.

"I know nothing of surgery," said Elizabeth, gratified at last to be asked what she knew, what she could do and could not do.

The dean interrupted her. "You do not mean to practice surgery!" He seemed altogether astonished.

"Why, of course she does!" broke in Dr. Webster with a look at Elizabeth that seemed to say, "Now let me show you how to handle this serious fellow."

He smiled, almost winked. "Think of the cases of femoral hernia. Only think what a well-educated woman would do in a city like New York!

"Why, my dear sir," he added, and Elizabeth could not be certain whether he was enthusiastic or joking, "she'd have her hands full in no time; her success would be immense!"

He turned to Elizabeth, his face shining with cordiality. "Yes, yes," he said, encouragingly, "you'll go through the course and get your diploma with the greatest *éclat*. We'll give you the opportunities. You'll make a stir, I can tell you!"

Although Elizabeth could see that it was the jovial little professor's nature to please everybody, she could not help feeling heartened.

In her diary she wrote that evening, "My first happy day!"

The little professor did everything merrily. She had given him, before asking for the privilege of entering his class, a letter of introduction written by her old friend Dr. Warrington. Elizabeth waited outside while he read the letter to the class. At one passage there were shouts of laughter. Dr. Warrington with his characteristic Quaker dignity had referred in his letter to the "age and experience" of the ruddy, jovial, roly-poly little professor.

"Gentlemen," Elizabeth could hear him saying when the noise had somewhat subsided. "With a lady in our midst we shall have to curb our masculine merriment."

The laughter and the shouts were louder than ever. The little professor, Elizabeth was later to learn, was a born jokester. It had been his habit to garnish his anatomical lectures with hearty jokes and medical anecdotes. Foot stamping, huzzas and whistlings were not at all uncommon in his class.

Under the influence of the merry little professor Elizabeth was greeted with handclappings when she entered the anatomy class, and although no one spoke to her, the atmosphere was altogether more friendly now.

After the lesson, the anatomy demonstrator, tall, lanky Mr. Fields, who had shut her out from the dissection room before, came over and at Dr. Webster's request made plain some points in the lessons she had missed.

The little professor came up to interrupt. "You attract altogether too much attention, Miss Blackwell," he said.

She looked at him, surprised.

But he smiled at her, as usual mischievously, and seemed to be enjoying himself. "There were a large number of strangers present this afternoon at my lecture."

And indeed, the townspeople, hearing that Elizabeth had finally been admitted to the classes, were clamoring now for visitor's tickets. A newspaper writer had been present too, coming all the way from Springfield, Massachusetts. And the following week the article appeared.

"She is a pretty little specimen of the feminine gender," the reporter had written. "She comes into the class with great composure, takes off her bonnet and puts it under the seat, exposing a fine phrenology." The effect of the new student on the class, a subject on which there had been great speculation, had been amazingly good, the paper admitted. "Great decorum is observed while she is present."

Little boys clambered on the bricks, hung by their finger tips, frightened and excited eyes peeped over the window sills wherever she went. "I never walked abroad," wrote Elizabeth in her diary, "but hastening daily to my college as to a sure refuge, I knew when I shut the great doors behind me, that I shut out all unkindly criticism."

And the students soon accepted her. A trivial happening was to her, one day, the source of great gratification. Close to the medical college stood an old house which had been fitted out as a private school for young ladies. The windows of one of the lecture rooms at the college looked out over a low wall, directly into the windows of the young ladies' school. Usually the shades were decorously drawn there, but sometimes, from behind these shades there were peepings, whisperings, giggles.

Coming into this classroom one day, a few moments early, Elizabeth found all the young men at the windows, straining over each other's shoulders, pushing, laughing, calling out to the young women across the way, who were evidently peeping out from behind their screens.

"See, the one in pink!" "No, no!" another boy shouted, "Up there, the one in blue!" There was a whistle of approval as the one in blue lifted the screen and for an instant flirtatiously showed herself.

"Here, get out of the way, let me have a look!" There was a tussling at the window, a struggle, and then sudden silence as several of the boys became aware of Elizabeth's presence.

They became confused. "Oh!" But she smiled at them so gently, that in spite of themselves they grinned like small boys caught in some act of nonsense by a friendly, older sister.

And this was just the feeling she had for these boisterous, overgrown country boys. One day in the amphitheatre a dart came sailing from a boy with red hair, and moist, rosy lips. When she looked in the direction of the dart, lifting her eyes from her notebook, he winked.

Elizabeth flushed, bent her head. He had been showing off; the whole class was watching. When the second dart came sailing, she brushed it away. Then she heard a warning hiss behind her, and became aware gratefully that some of the other students were objecting, were actually taking her part! She was subjected to no further annoyance.

But she was glad all the same when she was changed to another anatomy section. Dr. Le Ford, the surgeon, selected four of the steadier students to work with her in a small room adjoining the amphitheatre.

The demonstrations took place in the amphitheatre where a place in the first tier of seats was always reserved for Elizabeth. Dr. Webster, the lecturer, was a voluble and exciting teacher indeed. After his talk, which was given in the evening about seven o'clock, lamps were lit in the dissection chambers and the work there could continue as long as anyone wished to stay.

Elizabeth was always one of the last ones to leave, working silently and intently with the young men at her table. They kept on their hats while at work and handed and took the instruments which they exchanged with each other without any comment. "Blackwell," they called her, as though she might have been a man. And each time they spoke her name in this professional, impersonal way, it seemed like a tribute—a tribute to everything that she had struggled for.

One day a disheartening incident occurred. When she got home after the day's lectures, Miss Waller handed her a letter. It bore the college insignia. Elizabeth tore it open anxiously and was surprised to find that Dr. Webster had written her, a formal and very serious note.

Phrasing the matter with the utmost tact, he asked Elizabeth to absent herself from the next day's lesson. "An operation of a very delicate nature will be performed," he wrote, and added that she would have plenty of opportunity to cover this part of her study in "unembarrassed privacy."

"It was the thought of the faculty," he continued, "that it would be disquieting for the lecturer and also for the students, to have a woman present."

Elizabeth sat down immediately to frame a reply. She wrote rapidly; that she was a registered student and had paid her full tuition, she reminded the professor, and pointed out also, that for this reason she was of course entitled to attend all the lectures and take part in all the demonstrations.

She paused for a moment, holding the pen. He would chuckle at this hard-headed insistence; she knew it would please the merry little professor to see that she could stand up for her rights, and could demand what was owing her!

Then she went on to write more seriously. "All parts of the human body," she said, "are holy within the sight of God. Nor are the pangs of disease biased.

"To this end," she continued, "it is the duty of the physician, as you yourself have taught me, to study with equal reverence all the wonders of the body and all the illnesses to which it is subject."

She closed the letter humorously. If the professor would really be embarrassed by the presence of a lady on the first tier of seats, she would gladly take her place in the upper row, where neither he nor the rest of the class would have to be aware of her presence.

As to her own feelings, which he had suggested this absence might spare, "the physician who is not afraid of death, must certainly not be afraid of the body in life, or of any of its manifestations."

The next morning she waited in the anteroom to the lecture room, while Professor Webster, who had received her letter, read it to the class. "They shall make the decision," he said, and seemed very much moved at what she had written.

When the door opened finally, and at his nod she entered the amphitheatre, the young men rose, and standing before their seats, they gave her an ovation. Her lips trembled and her eyes were full of tears.

The next day Dr. Webster sent a student to summon

Elizabeth. A patient had been brought to his rooms, and he asked that Miss Blackwell be present at the examination. Only second-term students were accorded such a privilege; but this, she felt, was his answer to her letter.

He explained the case to Elizabeth. A farm boy had injured his finger on the edge of a rusty rake. The wound had festered, and now blood poisoning had set in, the angry red streaks showing on the arm, which was swollen and hot and very painful.

He showed Elizabeth how to make hot poultices and how to apply them. For two days she worked over the sick boy who lay on a cot in the doctor's study. And when he was ready to lance the wound, she was the only one chosen to be present.

Elizabeth walked home quietly that evening. It was cold and crisp outside with an early frost that had made the ground rigid. She drew a deep breath. The fresh air blowing up from the lake was good after the heavy smell of the sickroom.

She felt her way into the house and, without lighting her candle or the "airtight," without even putting away her books or her bonnet which she left where they fell, she took off her clothes and flung herself down on the bed.

At five o'clock in the morning she was awake, sitting up with the bedclothes bundled around her, copying out notes and studying for the monthly quiz. Anatomy, with all its inspiration, was also a drudgery. More than two hundred bones to memorize, four hundred muscles, besides nerves, blood vessels, glands. How could she memorize it all, and ever remember it? Walking to and from school she repeated the Greek and the Latin names, and hardly noticed that passers-by no longer stared at her, and no longer went to such pains to avoid her.

At the boarding house, too, it was much pleasanter. In Miss Waller she had found a real friend. She enjoyed the landlady's dry humor and her acrid almost wry manner, which hid all the same a very bountiful heart. When she came home late at night from dissections, she found a plate of bread and butter covered with a napkin in her room, and a pitcher of milk.

To say thank you for these was to get a cold look from Miss Waller, who always pretended that the Irish maid of all work was responsible. "I'm sure I don't know what nonsense that soft-hearted wench is up to."

The grim-visaged maiden lady, the boarder who had been so indignant at Elizabeth's presence at first, had also turned out to be quite a friendly person in spite of her gruffness. As for her timid sister, Amelia Walker, the one with the waterfall and the plaintive frightened voice, Elizabeth was very much gratified to have this lady ask her one day if she knew a cure for a headache.

"My first conquest and my first patient," Elizabeth wrote home to her mother.

But all the same Elizabeth kept very much to herself. However, it was pleasant to know that she was no longer hated or looked on as an insane or dangerous person.

"The people at first regarded me with suspicion," she had written in her diary. "But in Geneva the nine days' wonder soon will cease, and I cannot but congratulate myself on having found at last the right place for my beginning."

At the school there was a bustle of excitement, preparatory to the mid-winter holiday, when most of the students would go to their homes. But for Elizabeth, for whom it would have meant a week of travel by stagecoach, steamboat, and rail, it was quite impossible to think of such a thing. She planned to work on her notes and study, and for this reason went to call on Dr. Webster one day, asking him to outline some holiday work for her.

"I think," he said, when he had made some suggestions, "that when the term closes in February, you should attempt to get in somewhere for actual clinical practice."

She looked at him. "Where?"

"You have friends in Philadelphia, and you have courage too. You might well be the first woman to become a junior resident at Blockley."

"At the almshouse?"

He smiled. "The thought doesn't frighten you, does it?"

She gave him a thoughtful look. "No."

At once she wrote a letter to her friend, Dr. Elder, and a note too to kind Dr. Warrington to whom she had not written for some time.

"Dear Friend:" she wrote, "it is now almost Christmas, and the season of lectures will soon be over. Impossible as this hope may seem to you, I am desirous of entering the hospital of Blockley Almshouse this summer as a junior resident. May I ask once more for your help?"

Christmas came. She ate almonds and raisins in her room alone, read over the "Family Annual," a savory of happenings at home, prepared each year under the editorship of her able sister Marion; and allowed herself the luxury of a spell of homesickness.

To the Annual every member of the family had contributed. Her brother Henry had sent an abolitionist verse, a copy of one of his poems that had been printed in the Cincinnati paper. Elizabeth smiled. The prosperity of the hardware business did not please him half so much as the smallest public approval of the causes for which, like his father before him, he worked so ceaselessly.

"I shall work for the freedom of women," he wrote to his sister, "as I have worked for the freedom of the enslaved Negro race." And he made some comment about the eloquent speaker on feminine causes, whom he had met again in the home of Harriet Beecher Stowe.

He was referring, of course, to Lucy Stone. "Our son is a most eager disciple of this inspiring young orator," her mother had written, whose contribution to the Annual was a commentary on everybody's affairs.

An original song and a drawing had come from Anna,

who wrote again of her hope to "get somehow to Paris";
and from Emily, who was still teaching and was still discontented, came a long communication on her hopes of becoming a doctor, *too*. "I will follow you," she wrote to Elizabeth.

Emily, gentle but stubborn, had always followed Elizabeth. They had tumbled under fences together, had eaten
out of the same porridge bowl in the nursery, and later had
cut their gowns from the same pattern. But always it was
Elizabeth who was the initiator, curly-haired Emily who
was the follower.

On New Year's day the sound of voices and skates rang
out from the lake. From her room Elizabeth could both see
and hear the skaters. But all day she stayed at her desk,
wrapped in a shawl because the day was very cold, and
wrote steadily. When the skaters were gone and the town
was quite dark, she went down to the post with her letters
—letters of petition to the directors and the members of the
board of Blockley Almshouse!

CHAPTER FIVE

*N*O, MADAM, NO! FOR YOUR OWN GOOD I MUST
tell you it's quite impossible. Believe me, Blockley Almshouse is no place for a woman."

And trying to be reasonable, the director of Philadelphia's
almshouse explained once more that he himself was liberal,
but it would be ruinous in so far as his political career was
concerned, to recommend a woman as a junior resident at
Blockley.

"Why the worst criminals are here, the vagrants, the very
scum of the earth. How can I suggest that any woman well
brought up and well trained should be exposed to such an
atmosphere?"

"But," said Elizabeth, "I'm trained as a physician. What these people are cannot matter to me. What matters to me is that they're ill, and that working at Blockley, like any other medical student, I may gain the experience to help them. . . ."

The director interrupted her. "Madam," he said, "maybe you can forget your sex—we cannot!"

He got up, was about to open the door, but Elizabeth stopped him.

"Mr. Gilpin," she said, "have you ever had an insurmountable difficulty to face?"

He looked at her. "Insurmountable! I don't recognize the word." He puffed out his cheeks. "I always get what I want."

"That's what I thought," replied Elizabeth. "If you'll forgive me, that's just the quality I recognized, the very first time I came here to see you."

The director looked at her curiously, and as though for the first time. He smiled.

"Although I'm not a man," Elizabeth went on, tugging thoughtfully at her glove, "I have a little of that quality myself. I thought you would recognize it, and sensing how similar we were, I felt certain you would help me."

She held out her hand. "I still think so," she declared with a smile.

"Perhaps I can do something," said the director and seemed surprised at himself. He held open the door for her to pass. "You understand I objected, madam," he went on almost apologizing, "only because I had your best interests at heart."

"I understand," said Elizabeth.

Two weeks later she received a letter informing her of her admission to the almshouse as a resident. Her period of service was to be four months.

Dr. Elder congratulated her. But Mrs. Elder, who had brought her the letter, was not so encouraging. "I wonder," she said, "if you realize, if you can possibly imagine what you're getting into."

The almshouse, situated beyond the river, at the outskirts of the city, in a region of bleak and desolate meadows, was grim enough even from the outside. Four massive buildings, a quadrangle of stone, guarded by a high, unpainted fence, an iron gate, a gatekeeper's cupola. And here more than a thousand sick and poor were housed: orphans, aged folks, vagrants, the victims of fever. It was both a poorhouse and a hospital, shunned by good citizens and ravaged by the greed of politicians. But for students of medicine there could be no better laboratory.

Elizabeth was assigned to the women's department, a vast ward on the third floor of the hospital proper.

Her room, adjacent to the ward, was clean, but she was at first much disturbed by the sights and sounds of the hospital, and by the curiosity and unfriendliness of the patients.

Those who could walk would gather about her door. "A woman doctor! What strange sort of animal could that be?" They were forever spying and peeking into the keyhole.

Elizabeth placed her table with its books and papers in line with the keyhole. When this did not satisfy their curiosity she opened the door wide and wrote after that in full view of anyone who wanted to watch her. Naturally the peekings and the whisperings soon stopped. But it was a long time before Elizabeth gained the confidence of her patients, who eyed her slyly as one would a freak.

One old woman would not permit Elizabeth to come near her bed. "It is not fitting," she said, and clung to the Bible she was constantly reading. "Women can cook and women can sew. They can nurse and they can tend those who are ailing . . ."

But she refused to believe that a woman could be a doctor.

"I may be poor and cast by the Lord to a pauper's lot," she complained in a high, querulous, self-righteous voice, "but I'll have no such woman to take care of me in my illness."

Elizabeth, who had received a very good jar of calf's-foot jelly from Mrs. Elder, one day casually left the gift on the old woman's table. The jelly disappeared and so did the jar, but after that she had no more trouble with this patient.

"There are more paths than one . . ." Elizabeth wrote to her mother, to whom she never confided a difficulty until it was solved.

The head surgeon and his assistants treated Elizabeth kindly enough, but the other junior residents were not only cold to her, they caused her actual trouble!

One morning a particularly trying incident occurred. It was Elizabeth's duty, on her morning visits, to see that the day's medicine had been dispensed. In order to do this it was necessary for her to read the chart of directions which hung at the head of each patient's bed.

At the first bed at which she stopped, she saw that this chart was missing. The patient, a young girl with a sly expression, looked pleased.

Elizabeth felt under the pillow at once, thinking the girl had secreted it.

"Where is the chart?" Her voice was stern.

"The gentleman doctor took it away. He took them all!" The girl's sly look had deepened. And Elizabeth, glancing around, saw that every chart in the ward was missing!

This was the work of the junior residents, who took every means to embarrass her work and humiliate her before the patients. When she walked into a ward, they showed her quite plainly what they thought of women as doctors. To a man they would walk out without a word! And now they had maliciously removed the charts.

The girl on the bed was looking at Elizabeth out of the corner of her eye, waiting with relish for an explosion of temper.

But Elizabeth only sighed, turned down the covers and

looked at the girl's wound, an ulcer just below the knee which was stubbornly refusing to heal.

"It's no better," said the sick girl. The petulant lips trembled. "I will never get better!" And all the bitterness she had wanted to vent on Elizabeth gave way now in a flood of tears.

Elizabeth sat down beside her and waited until she had stopped crying. "Well," she said, "do you feel better now?"

The girl smiled. Her furtive expression was gone. "The charts," she said, "are stuffed away in that closet by the window."

"Don't worry about that," said Elizabeth.

But she was glad to have the charts back again, because she had very much disliked the thought of going to the surgeon in charge of the wards. That evidently was just what the other students wanted her to do, since it would show that she couldn't handle her own problems, and couldn't get along in the wards.

On the next bed sat an old woman, very neat in an old faded gown much too big for her. She was the widow of a carpenter and since she was rapidly going blind and had no one to take care of her, she had been sent to the hospital.

As Elizabeth turned, she puckered her lips and began complaining. Her voice was timid. It was like the complaint of a child.

Elizabeth took the old woman's hand. The cold fingers curled up in her palm like a child's.

"Here I am, Grandmother," she said, and listened again to the stories the old woman quavered out about her good husband, about the neat home she had kept.

After a while, Elizabeth persuaded her to drink the medicine she had neglected, and to eat the dark bread that she had left over from her dinner, although this really should have been the concern of the nurses.

The nurses at Blockley were vicious and ignorant. Many of them were former inmates of the almshouse, or else they were charwomen who couldn't get work and so were willing, for the very low wages that were paid, to nurse the sick.

Nurse Welch, in charge of the women's ward, was surly and impertinent, and at first very unfriendly to Elizabeth. She was a big woman with black eyes, a tremendous bosom, powerful hands. She could pick up a mattress and turn it in her arms. And she handled the patients without any thought for their comfort, scolding and nagging all the while if no physician was near to stop her.

She made constant visits to the bakehouse in the yard, where the wines were kept which were sometimes prescribed as stimulants for the very sick. And each time she came back her nose was more red and her voice was more arrogant.

"What a pity," thought Elizabeth, when she heard Nurse Welch's rough quarrelsome voice, "that sick people should be left in her care."

Although Elizabeth had often heard it said that gentlewomen would never stoop to caring for the sick, she began now to agree with her friend, Dr. Warrington, who said that only good women, properly trained, should be nurses. In fact, this amazing old man had gathered together in his home a number of young women from the very finest families of the city and was instructing them in the art of what he called "scientific nursing." He had even written a book, *The Nurses' Guide* and had founded a club which he called The Philadelphia Nurses Society.

Of course these young women only went out to nurse in private families and in the best of homes. But some day, Dr. Warrington predicted, there would be nurses who would be willing to go out and take care of anyone—even in a public almshouse, or in a charity hospital!

Elizabeth had heard her friend called a fanatic and an insane person, for entertaining such views. But as she saw how roughly and how poorly the sick were cared for at Blockley, she became convinced that the old Quaker physician was doing a very great work.

She dreamed of the day when she might found her own hospital where the sick would be taken care of sympathetically and kindly. And another hope grew in her mind. When she became a physician, she decided, she would devise some plan for teaching her patients how to live at home and how to take care of themselves.

"There ought to be home visitors," she said to herself, "who will see that sickness is prevented before it starts!" But this idea seemed so farfetched, so far from practicality that she hadn't the courage to confide it to anyone.

Besides, who was there to tell? She went very seldom now to call on the Elders, although she would have enjoyed Dr. Elder's encouragement and his wife's scolding, disapproving kindness. But visits to the city were almost out of the question. The junior residents had to be "on call" for weeks at a time. Besides, if she did have "leave," the trip to the home of her friends by ferryboat and omnibus was too tedious and tiring after a day in the wards.

She was always tired now and not half so vigorous as she had been on entering. For one thing, she found it difficult to eat. The food was coarse and badly cooked and the other students in the dining room were not only unfriendly, they were rude, turning away when she came in, and never addressing themselves to her.

She choked down her meals, and what she couldn't eat she would smuggle out in her napkin, to give to the nurse in the children's ward, for some ailing or delicate child. But she had a very strong suspicion that the nurse ate this food herself, for once she had caught her standing in a corner, munching.

How anyone could eat in the fetid atmosphere of the wards, where the windows were never opened and even the walls seemed to give out odors, Elizabeth could never understand.

She had been warned jokingly by Dr. Elder about the almshouse smell.

> "You may scrub, you may ventilate
> the wards as you will,
> But the smell of the almhouse
> will cling to you still."

It was a smell compounded of the exhalations of sick, unwashed bodies, the steam from stale cooking, and the sweetish, sharp odor of medicines, unguents and plasters. It penetrated food, clothing, even the papers and books in her room. And it seemed to cling to her fingers, her clothes, her hair.

After the dressing tour with the surgeon, one morning, Elizabeth went to her room, very discouraged. The patients had been irritable, the doctor sharp, and the other student residents had treated her as usual with coldness.

She opened the windows, looking out on the fields which to her surprise were not gray like the walls around her, but green and fresh, in spite of the heat. It had gotten warm early, and the air in the hospital was oppressive. "Fine weather," an old pauper woman had said, "for breeding a fever." And there was always talk in the wards about typhus and cholera, the two diseases which each summer took such a toll of the poor people and the vagrants shut up in the almshouse. And how could it be otherwise when their food was so miserable and their care so inadequate?

"Do not fear for me," Elizabeth had written to her mother. "I go on smoothly and healthily at Blockley; there is nothing pestilential among the diseases, and I live simply, do my duty, trust in God, and mock at the devil!"

But she was becoming deeply affected by the suffering and misery around her. Standing in the corridor, one evening, when the late dressings were over, and the out wards had been locked up for the night, she felt too listless, almost too discouraged to go to her room and study.

A consumptive woman coughed down the hall. Somewhere, feebly, a child was wailing, and from time to time through the open door of the ward came the sound of heavy breathing.

She went into her room, thrust open the window, washed her face, poured cold water over her arms, and with resolution sat down to make notes. But she broke off suddenly and began to write to her mother.

"All this is horrible!" she wrote. "Women must really open their eyes to it. I am convinced that they must regulate this matter. But how!"

She was present in the wards before breakfast time, saw the grayish bowls of tea, the hard bread made from middlings. No wonder that scurvy flourished! She had heard that while the sick and poor lacked blankets, the steam yacht of the political boss would be drawn up at the dock to be stocked with coal, provisions and liquors.

She went restlessly to her own breakfast. In the steward's dining room she sat alone. But this morning she was quite indifferent.

After the surgeon's visit to the wards, she took up a light shawl. Although the morning was bright, she felt chilly, permeated with the gloom of the corridors. She passed through the narrow, shelterless yard where some paupers stood around apathetically, and an old soldier who had fought with Napoleon at Leipzig talked to himself, flourishing his cap and making gestures with a stick.

At the gate between the men's out wards and the hospital, a fat politician presided. He had once been a saloonkeeper in the old Navy Yard and had promised Elizabeth one day that if she ever managed to open an office he would send her all of his friends.

"There is not a thief, a gambler or a thug in the whole

district of Southwark," he had said proudly, "who isn't my friend!"

He was wedged in his little house, so fat that he could not get up without a stick. Although he smiled and waved to her, Elizabeth avoided him this morning.

She turned quickly toward the river. The sun was warm here. She sat down on a stone, let the shawl slip from her shoulders, and for a long time sat watching the brown water slipping in and out among the piles.

After a time her head dropped forward, and for about five minutes she must have slept, because when she opened her eyes again she was quite refreshed. For some reason she remembered a bit of advice that Dr. Warrington had given her.

"Thee must not stay too much within those gray walls." And then looking down at her he had added, "I know that thy nature is ardent."

For all of his Quaker ways, this kind old physician was ardent himself, thought Elizabeth, or else he would not have known of her own inclination to drive herself.

"I am indeed more a doer than a thinker," Elizabeth had once written in her diary. But at Blockley, in spite of the long hours of ward work and study, she had more occasion for thinking than she had ever had in her life.

As she sat by the river, the memory of yesterday afternoon's operations was vividly with her. The amphitheatre, she had been surprised to see, was dark and poorly ventilated. All around the walls were cases of pathologic specimens in greasy, unpleasant containers.

The surgeon, a tall man with a full, carelessly-kept beard, came in, took off his coat, turned up his sleeves, pinned an ordinary huckaback towel over his waistcoat.

The patient was brought in. He seemed to Elizabeth to be some kind of dock worker or laborer, because his clothes were stained and his hands were grimy. With a frightened smile he sat down in the surgeon's chair, and with the help of one of the assisting students he drew off his coat, loosened his clothes at the neck, and when the surgeon spoke to him, he pulled his shirt down over his shoulder, exposing the angry red gathering of a carbuncular growth.

When the surgeon touched him he winced. The students were allowed to come forward and view the site of the operation, each student making notes. Elizabeth came last and would have spoken to the big, frightened fellow, but knew that she shouldn't, and was quite relieved when he was given a tall glass of laudanum and wine to drink. Spirits of ether, that new sleeping medicine which could be inhaled from a handkerchief, would not be wasted on such a rough and poor patient!

On the table stood a big bowl of sponges, an old pitcher for rinsing the instruments. The surgeon began explaining the nature of the operation. In the buttonhole of his coat were several silk threads ready for sewing the wound. As he talked, he resined these sewing threads with beeswax, holding one end of the thread in his mouth and the other end in his fingers. Then the operation began.

At the first flow of blood, a distressing thing happened. One of the students who was sitting close to the patient, got up, wavered and was about to faint. Elizabeth had seen this happen once before in the operating amphitheatre, and had been surprised at that time over the lack of sympathy on the part of the other students.

They showed the same attitude again. "Soft stomach! Go home to Mamma!" they taunted. And somehow amidst whispered jeers, the boy got to the door and outside.

Elizabeth was indignant. "You should be ashamed of yourself!" she said to the boy next to her, who looked surprised. It was the first time she had spoken to any of the resident students, or to any of the hospital assistants.

For the head physician of the almshouse, she had a great admiration. How a man like Dr. Nathan Dow Benedict came to be appointed to an institution ruled by politics, she could hardly understand. He had fine features full of restraint, and gray eyes that were as gentle almost as a woman's. Elizabeth had seen tears come into his eyes as he bent over a dying child!

But for all his softness, he could be stern too. He fought ceaselessly for better food for the inmates, saying that a quarter of a pound of old meat a day, weak tea, and poor bread, with an occasional trickle of fourth-grade molasses, was no food for the sick, even for the indigent poor.

Never hurried, always ready to listen to complaints, he was everywhere at once, in the wards, at the weekly clinics. He had time, too, even for the children's corridor crowded with offcasts, where Elizabeth liked to follow him.

More than a hundred children were crowded into one long room at the end of the hospital. Pale, puny, apathetic, underfed, there was no place for them to exercise, nor were there toys for them to play with. Every few days another child was stricken with ophthalmia, that dreadful disease of the eyes which is carried from one child to another by dirty towels and common basins.

Sometimes a sick child would cry at night. Elizabeth in her room would awaken. In the whole hospital there were no nurses at night, only the watchman with his stick who, under the dim, smoking lamps, would make his rounds hourly through the dim, gloomy corridors.

Often Elizabeth had the impulse to get up, go into the children's ward, comfort a sick child. To some of the children she had brought sugarplums and cookies from the box that her mother sent her. But what could she do with one box when there were a hundred sick semi-starved children who needed caring for!

One little girl, Mary-Jane, followed Elizabeth around through the hospital wherever she went, and once came at night to her room. "I don't want to sleep alone," she said. And Elizabeth, disregarding the regulations, took the little girl into her bed. From a corncob and a piece of gingham she made a doll for the child. After that, the two, Mary-Jane and her corncob baby, were never separated.

Elizabeth had made only one friend at the hospital, the matron, who ruled in an immense room in the center of the almshouse proper. In a starched dress, a white cap over her smooth gray hair, she sat in an imposing armchair with her feet propped up on a velvet footstool.

In spite of this imposing position, she was busy and harassed from night until morning, dispensing orders incessantly, giving out clothing, calling for linens, accounting for supplies, ordering unruly paupers to the bath, adjudging quarrels, censuring a greedy nurse, scolding a careless watchkeeper. There was a great deal of stealing and cheating among the nurses and the watchkeepers, who were fully capable of drinking up the precious potions of wine left for dying patients.

Both kindly and hot-tempered, this strong-minded woman arranged everything, saw everything, and managed everyone from the top steward to the lowest porter. She was shrewd, overlooked the graft of the directors when she had to, lied if it was necessary, scolded fiercely, or else over a cup of tea told Elizabeth of the comforts she found in her religion.

Sometimes, though, this kind and religious woman could be as Elizabeth described her in a letter, "a very Mrs. Beelzebub."

One day as Elizabeth came in, she found her shaking a half-witted girl, an inmate who helped in the wards for the female aged. The girl sobbed. She had stolen food, secreting it in a hole in the wall, so that there were mice in the ward, and the housekeeper could not clean them out.

When the girl had gone, the matron turned to Elizabeth. "There, you see, I've lost my temper again!" And she seemed to be excusing herself. Then she smoothed her apron, straightened her cap, and taking out her keys she opened the little cabinet above the table, and locking the door she prepared to serve tea to her visitor.

These were pleasant hours for Elizabeth and she looked forward to them. But today the matron was tired and distracted.

The ship fever had come, she announced gloomily. Two cases in the men's ward. She looked into her teacup and then at Elizabeth. "Soon we shall have them lying in all the corridors!"

She was referring to petechial typhus, the dreadful summer disease which every year ravaged Philadelphia's poor, and which was brought in usually by the immigrant ships coming from Ireland.

The next day Elizabeth went to Dr. Benedict to discuss with him the subject of her thesis for the season's work. It was customary for the students to write about some disease they had seen and studied during their summer's residency.

He was stern and preoccupied. "You could write of typhus," he said. She looked at him astonished, having somewhat discounted the words of the matron.

"There will soon be more at hand than we have beds for!" And he told Elizabeth that in the night several more sick had been brought in from the same ship. "It's a disease of misery and filth," he said.

And now there was an air of foreboding and expectancy in the hospital. The resident students, harassed by the long hours of ward work and the ceaseless influx of patients, had no time to be hostile now. They spoke to Elizabeth, forgetting in their fatigue and added responsibility the grudge that they had formerly borne her because she was a woman.

Elizabeth was glad for this notice, impersonal as it was, for she had no friend to whom she could address herself now. The matron was too busy to invite her to tea any more. Beds had to be carried down from the attics, bed ticks had to be filled with fresh straw, and every day fresh supplies of calomel, scammony, aloes, quinine and opium had to be brought up from the pharmacy for the sick patients.

From her mother, who had read in the papers about the gathering epidemic, Elizabeth got an anxious letter. While Mrs. Blackwell didn't ask that Elizabeth should leave her post, certainly she inferred she would be happy to know that she was in safer surroundings.

"I have chosen my work," Elizabeth replied, and then added reassuringly, "I assure you, kindest Mother," she said, "that I am well taken care of and am in no danger."

It did not occur to her for one moment that she could be taken ill. "I haven't the time for it," she said when she heard that one of the other young residents had taken sick and was dying.

Soon the wards were all filled, and finally even the corridors were lined to the doorways with cots that stood end to end. The sickness came on suddenly: chills, a pain in the head, an aching all over the body as in the case of a cold, then fever and delirium.

Cupping was prescribed, and blood-letting and leeching. In extreme cases, the fever patients were doused with cold water.

"A fever is a fire," said Dr. Benedict, who had grown very thin under the strain of his work, "and water puts out a fire."

Sometimes this strenuous remedy helped. But no one knew what caused the dreadful fever with its accompanying brown eruption, and no one knew how to cure it.

In the children's wards, where the disease had likewise raged, it was milder. Very few children died. But among the middle-aged and the elderly, out of every four who fell sick, one patient was taken, and those who survived lay listless for weeks, sometimes months.

By August it was necessary to open the pest house, a rough board building near the Potter's Field. And still new patients came!

At night Elizabeth, often too tired to sleep, sat with her face in her hands over her study table. But she could not work on her thesis. How courageously she had written down the title, *The Causes and Treatment of Typhus, or Ship-fever*. Yet when all was written and said what did any physician really know about this sickness?

Where did the disease come from? What caused it? How could it be conquered? She began to recollect each case she had attended, and taking out the voluminous notes she had kept, decided that she would include them. This was better than any theory from books. And she began to write rapidly, noting down what she had seen and experienced.

By September the epidemic had subsided. The long rows of beds had disappeared from the corridors, and in the wards many beds that had been occupied were empty.

All day there was whitewashing and painting going on. Under the matron's scolding directions, doors and windows were scrubbed, beds scalded, mattresses aired and put into fresh ticks. But the almshouse smell remained.

It was now almost a natural atmosphere to Elizabeth, and sitting in her room over the first fire, she looked out on the autumn sunset and could say to herself that she regretted to leave.

Elizabeth took out from her box, the next day, her heavy black frock faced with satin. "This," she said to Mary-Jane, who was sitting at the window with her corncob doll, "is the dress I shall wear when I graduate."

"Graduate?" The child looked at her.

"When I become a doctor, next year."

"Like Dr. Benedict?" Mary-Jane could think of nothing better.

Elizabeth smiled. "Well," she said, "not exactly like him. Not for a very long time . . ." She shook out the folds of the dress and hung it up before the window to air.

Mary-Jane fingered it. "Will I have a dress like this some-day?"

"Someday," said Elizabeth, "you shall be a fine woman, and you shall have a fine dress!"

In the evening she put on the gown, and having arranged her hair smoothly over her cheeks, she took up her thesis and went with it to Dr. Benedict's quarters in the main building.

She had worked very hard on the paper, into which she had put all her observations of the epidemic and of the patients she had attended. The head surgeon on reviewing her thesis had asked that she come to his office and read it— before the other junior residents.

They were sitting at the long conference table in Dr. Benedict's study, and when he arose as she entered, being almost old-fashioned in his courtesy, they got up too.

She took her place in the chair that was empty, at the right hand of the doctor's, and while he spoke she kept her head bowed, not daring to look up at the young men who had worked with her so grudgingly, and who had caused her so much heartache.

The room was silent as he began. "When Miss Blackwell arrived, the first woman to enter Blockley Almshouse, as a junior resident," he said, "I, too, was skeptical.

"I had seen strong young men, who came here and could not bear to stay.

"But she did. Her work has been good and during our late troubles she did not once become frightened and did not once spare herself.

"She has written a sound thesis, full of the painstaking observations of the careful physician. I am going to ask you gentlemen to listen while she reads you her work."

There was silence at the table and then applause. Elizabeth, who was struggling with herself, did not for an instant dare to look up.

Then she unfolded her paper and began in a very small voice to read. When she had finished there were questions and discussion. She forgot her timidity, and the young men around her seemed to have forgotten their resentment.

And when one of the junior residents, a very serious fellow, and one who had worked very hard during the epidemic, spoke to her informally and in a tone of professional comradeship, she turned to him with an almost radiant face.

"Blackwell," he said, "in that last case you described . . ."

She smiled. "I will be very glad to give you my notes, Doctor," she answered.

When it was all over and she was gathering up her papers, one of the young men who had been particularly cold to her, came up and held out his hand.

"Forgive me, Dr. Blackwell," he said, "I am certain you will someday make a fine physician."

When she realized that he was referring to the episode of the charts, they both laughed.

"Well," she said, "a good doctor should know the symptoms from the patient, and not," she added smiling, "from the charts!"

Before she left Philadelphia she went to call on the Elders, of course, who kept her talking for hours about all that had happened during the summer. Now that it was over she could speak almost humorously to her friends. They sat in the parlor listening, and Dr. Elder, holding her thesis in his hands, read what she had written.

When he was through he got up, put his hand on her shoulders, and was about to speak, when his wife interrupted him.

"That's all very well," she said in her complaining fond way, "but look how thin she's become!"

And, indeed, during the summer Elizabeth had grown thinner. But she was stronger, too, in a way that it was hard for her to describe.

"The excitement is gone and the fear, too," she wrote to her mother. "I feel like a physician."

CHAPTER SIX

THE RETURN TO SCHOOL, IN THE AUTUMN, was like a homecoming. In the long corridors, the young men greeted Elizabeth.

Some had been away on the farms of their parents, but a few, like Elizabeth, had been at work in neighboring hospitals.

They compared notes and cases. All were eager to hear about the typhus epidemic and about Elizabeth's experiences at Blockley.

Dr. Webster, as Elizabeth's adviser, looked over the thesis she had written during the summer. "Capital! Capital!" he said, and insisted on reading the paper at his opening class.

There were cries of "Hear! Hear!" and applause.

"Ladies and gentlemen," Dr. Webster began, and could not help making a speech. He reviewed the strange events of Elizabeth's coming, and told of the progress she had made.

With a feeling of deep satisfaction, Elizabeth bent her head over her notebook. Even the town seemed less unfriendly. The lady student was no longer a curiosity. "The nine days' wonder has ceased!" she wrote in her diary. The little boys had stopped their name-calling, and the men and women were tired of staring.

On her return to her lodgings, wry Miss Waller had invited her to an oyster supper in the kitchen, quite a privilege for a mere boarder, and the two maiden ladies had also asked politely after her health.

From home Elizabeth heard that her eldest sister Anna had achieved her ambition. She was leaving for Paris as writer for several important American papers.

Before leaving Anna had written warmly to her sister. "If your medical studies would benefit, perhaps you would join me here!"

Paris! The medical center of the world. Elizabeth went for a talk with the little, round, jolly anatomy professor, who received her quite seriously.

"There could be nothing better," he said, "but I doubt that the Parisian hospitals would under any circumstances admit a woman!"

Elizabeth was thoughtful. "I shall graduate first, get the money, and then we shall see."

The next day she assisted Dr. Webster at an operation. And when it was over and they were washing their hands, she confided that there was no part of her medical studies which was so fascinating to her as surgery.

He looked at her fingers. "You have deft and capable hands," he said, "small, and yet they're the hands of a surgeon." He told her not to strain and stiffen her fingers, not to carry heavy parcels or to do coarsening work.

"You must keep your hands pliable," he said, and he told her of exercises for relaxing the fingers.

And another time when she sat in the study hall bent over her books, he came up to her. "You're all the same," he almost shouted, for he had a temper too, "wasting your eyesight, which is the most precious thing that a surgeon possesses!"

Later Elizabeth learned that Dr. Webster, who was operating less frequently, was troubled with failing eyesight, and that despite his jollity this was a source of great bitterness to him.

And Elizabeth, who sat up late every night now studying the reports of famous operations, began to realize how important her eyes and her fingers were.

At the dissection table, one day, a little liquid spurted into her face. Elizabeth reached up to wipe it with the corner of her apron.

"Guard your eyes!" shouted Dr. Webster, and he gave her hand a blow, afterward apologizing.

"Without your eyes," he said, "your fingers are blind!" And as if he had said more than he wanted to, he strode from the room, coming back later to joke and banter as he passed from table to table in his usual informal way.

But on Elizabeth his comment had made a deep impression. And the students who had noticed Dr. Webster's concern for her, began to treat Elizabeth with a new respect and a greater sense of friendliness.

She began now to feel herself part of the school, taking part in all the events and excitements that transpired there.

The local Geneva paper had for some time been printing excited editorials about slavery and its extension, a matter that everybody discussed. In the school the students took sides, very vehemently, and so did the instructors.

Late in the month a noted Whig orator and a prominent

Democrat came to town for a public debate. The question was one about which everybody was excited. Should the new Missouri Territory be admitted into the Union as a slave state or as a free state?

The people who were in favor of slavery said, "Let the new state be slave." This was natural since they wanted a majority for their side. And the Northerners, wishing the free states to predominate, declared that under no circumstances must slavery be allowed in the new territory.

There was so much excitement in the school over this question, that on the day of the debate, classes were dismissed early. The speakers appeared. There was a torch rally and the inevitable street fights which greeted the discussion of this question in any city. And the next day, the students at the college held a class meeting to decide how the school stood on the matter, whether for freedom or slavery.

All the instructors attended and stood in the back of the room. Elizabeth, who was usually not of an excitable nature, felt nervous. She was particularly aware of the presence of the surgeon—Dr. Corydon Le Ford—whom she greatly admired, but whom she knew to be a follower of the slave-holding theory.

The evening before he had stopped her in the hallway and had spoken to her, attempting to dissuade her from her "Free Soil" leanings. Now, catching her glance, he looked at her significantly. Being of strong political inclinations, it was very important to him how the school declared itself.

But when Elizabeth's name was called, last of all, she stood up and took her place on the Free Soil side, making a majority for that group!

What a shouting, and tossing of caps, and foot stamping! "Good for you, Blackwell!" And the young men crowded around her shaking her hand. One young man, in his exuberance was about to thump her on the back, when he caught himself and thrusting his hands into his pockets, he grinned instead.

Elizabeth laughed, and so did the others. But in the hallway when Dr. Le Ford caught up with her she was instantly serious.

He seemed somewhat bitter. "I wonder," he said, "if politics is a matter for women?"

"If women can be doctors, why can't they vote!" It was the impudent, good-natured voice of Dr. Webster, behind them. Immediately there was an argument, the young men participating.

But Elizabeth, instead of being drawn into the controversy, only smiled, and turned in toward the classroom where she had left her books. She was not an orator for the rights of women, like her brother's friend, Lucy Stone.

Later she explained the matter to Miss Waller with whom she had grown quite friendly. "Every woman should do what she wants and what she is fitted for, and in no time at all we shall all have our opportunities."

After her studies in the evening, if it was not too late, she would come down to the kitchen, which was clean and unpretentious like the spare Scotswoman herself. Then the landlady would lay a plaid cloth on the scrubbed kitchen table, and they would sit over tea and bread and butter and cheese until Elizabeth would get up in alarm.

"If I don't go upstairs now," she would say, taking her cup to the wash basin, "then I shall surely meet myself coming down!"

Humming, she would dry the dishes, wash out the cloth, and hang it up to dry.

"If you didn't have that high-fangled notion of being a doctor," said the landlady dryly, "then you could have your board and your keep here any day as a kitchen maid."

"A much safer, and I think a much easier profession," laughed Elizabeth.

"Then you're really serious about going away to France

and becoming a surgeon?" The landlady seemed fascinated by this project of her boarder's. "Imagine, cutting people up and stitching them up again!"

"Oh," said Elizabeth, "I shall not only cut, I shall sew. I shall sew as beautifully as the good ladies of the Geneva Sewing Circle and Bible Society!"

And after this sociability, Elizabeth would go to her room again, and would study until the house grew so cold that she had to get into bed.

There were so many things that interested her besides the subjects she studied at school. One morning a student brought a new book to class, *The Vegetable Diet*. It was written by Dr. William A. Alcott, a cousin of Bronson Alcott, the lecturer. The whole Alcott family, it seemed, believed that meat was poison, and should not be eaten except by carnivorous animals.

The followers of this theory even went on to say that raw carrots and turnips were not only good food for rabbits, they were the best food a human being could eat. And instead of fine white bread, these "vegetarians" advised a coarse dark bread invented by a certain Dr. Sylvester Graham of Connecticut. It was called Graham bread.

Elizabeth read with interest how the wheat, just as it came from the fields, was ground up for this bread, and no parts, not even the husks, were thrown away.

She went to Dr. Webster eagerly. "It seems to me," she said, "that all the good of the wheat would be in such bread."

But he joked as usual. "Might as well eat the chicken with the feathers on!" And when she asked him if raw vegetables might not after all be better than when cooked, he looked at her skeptically at first. "Only people without appetites go in for such movements!" he said.

The result was a heated argument. "There's so much about the body that we don't know," said Elizabeth.

This was an opinion which had for some time been troubling her, and she couldn't help expressing it. After all, any kind of idea might have some good in it. "A good physician," she said, "should not be prejudiced. He should look everywhere . . ." Then she stopped abruptly, thinking she had offended the little doctor.

But instead of being angry he laughed. "Capital!" he cried out, "capital! You'll be a doctor yet!" And she heard him chuckling as she went down the hall.

What troubled her now, and had ever since she had been at Blockley, was the thought of the many diseases about which no one knew anything, not even the doctors.

There had been several cases of cholera reported in New York, and Dr. Charles Lee, in beginning his lectures on this subject, admitted that doctors could do very little—as a matter of fact, almost nothing for this disease.

"I wish I could tell you how to cure cholera," he said, "but under all modes of treatment the results are the same."

He admitted, almost complacently, that whether leeching, cupping, or blood-letting was employed, whether compresses were used, or medicines, the sickness seemed to run its course. Some patients got well, but many didn't.

"However," he added quite briskly, "I will tell you something of the disease, and what I would do if called to a case!"

Elizabeth communicated all this to Miss Waller, one evening, walking up and down heatedly in her kitchen.

"I should want to know more than that, and I will, if there's any human way to find out!" she said.

Some of the young men, who were being graduated in February, were already concerned with where they would rent offices and how they would get money for instruments.

But Elizabeth, who thought the eight months' course that was given quite inadequate, wrote to her sister in Paris.

"I am determined to come to you," she said. "I have studied enough to know that I know very little. Perhaps in the European schools I may learn more."

Her brother Henry, to whom she had also written about her great dissatisfaction, was entirely sympathetic.

"You have gone so far," he said, "we will help you to go further." And he promised again that he would lend her the money for the necessary studies, since what she had saved with her teaching was already gone.

In January, three weeks before graduation, the "green room" examinations were held. Elizabeth, like the others, came early the next morning and they stood around the bulletin board until the clerk came out with his long fluttering lists of paper and posted the results.

"There you are, Blackwell!" Her name stood high on the list.

Dr. Webster was pleased. "I told them so," he said, but he had a struggle on his hands nevertheless.

At the last faculty meeting a troublesome question had come up. For the first time in the history of medical education a woman had been allowed to study at a medical school. But could Geneva College go still further? Could they with propriety give a diploma to a member of the female sex?

The blunt little anatomy professor was fitted for just such a battle.

"She paid her tuition, didn't she? She passed every course, each and every one with honors! And let me tell you, gentlemen, if you hold back, I'll take up a campaign in every medical journal . . ."

And so by threats, cajoling, and worrying, the measure was passed. Miss Blackwell would receive her diploma with all the other members of the graduating class. On the 1849 roster of students her name was at last posted as a graduate!

The jolly little doctor, pointing out the list to her one day, made a joking comment. "It will become the fashion for ladies to become educated."

"Yes," replied Elizabeth, "like a new style in ladies' bonnets." But she strongly suspected that he had waged a battle in her behalf.

How could she ever thank this merry little man or show him her gratitude? Her heart swelled with appreciation. Then, as it happened, at the graduation she had to refuse what was for him an important request. He wanted her to march through the town with the graduates. She felt that she couldn't.

There was a great deal of excitement before the exercises, and Elizabeth was very glad that her brother Henry, always her favorite, had come to be with her.

He was tall and dignified in a new overcoat and a shining brown beaver. For the first time she showed herself in the town on the arm of a gentleman.

"You don't drape your shawl correctly," he said, "and your bonnet should have more of a poke." He fussed over her fondly. "My feeling of familism," he said proudly, "is strongly developed."

She kissed him, showed him her books, answered his enthusiastic and intelligent questions, and took him with her when she went to the school for the final oral examination.

He sat in an anteroom, his chin on his cane, and with great interest listened to the other students and their comments. A good deal of the talk was about his sister, whom the young men referred to informally as "our Elib," and "Lizzie." They had the friendliest feeling for her and all took a pride in what she had done.

"It seems to me," said Henry, later, as they were walking home, "that there is even some commotion of the heart in this!"

Elizabeth couldn't help laughing. "You're altogether too clever," she said, and couldn't help confiding that one of the young men had written her a letter asking for "the honor of an occasional correspondence," after she left school.

"Is that all?" Her brother seemed to be in a probing mood,

and thought of himself as quite an authority on such matters. "Is that all that our Blackwell ladies can do?"

"Now, Henry," she said, "you know that we're all as plain as hens, and very erratic besides. Whatever are you talking about?"

She did not tell her brother of an incident that had touched her. In the hallway, one of the older students had stopped her, the evening before, and rather shyly had told her that he was glad he had not graduated sooner, "Since," he said, "it gave me a chance to meet someone like you. You're not," he went on, "like any other girl I've ever known."

And Elizabeth, coming home that night, had looked in the mirror. A plain face, the nose somewhat bumpy, and straight, light hair combed down severely. How strange that the young man should have noticed her at all! And sighing, she got into bed, and began immediately to think of her work.

She would be almost glad when the excitement of the graduation was over, so that she could plan what she should do next, and how she should proceed.

On the morning of Commencement she got up early, and immediately Henry came to her door. He wanted to continue discussion of a question that had come up the evening before.

Dr. Webster, who with his jovial, open nature, was all for a public display, had insisted that she march in the Commencement parade. The medical school was located about a mile from the rest of the Geneva College campus, and it was the custom for the students, headed by the dignitaries of the college, to march from the medical building to the Literary Colleges.

The line of march passed along a wide avenue, the finest in town. And since very little happened in the village of Geneva, people came from far and wide, and in a great crush lined the streets on this occasion.

But what gave still greater interest to the event this year was the fact that a woman was graduating. What could be more exciting than to see this curious female? There had been a rush for tickets, and the several inns of the town were filled to capacity with visitors.

"You know what I think of Dr. Webster," said Elizabeth, "and how much I would like to please him. But I cannot see why he should desire that I should make a spectacle of myself."

She walked up and down the room in agitation. A note had come from the anatomy professor early that morning, and now another message arrived by messenger.

"No good would come of it," said Elizabeth. "Not for me nor for anyone else. Don't you see, Henry," she explained, "that no matter how persistent I've been, and how bold it was necessary to make myself sometimes, still I've gone at my work quietly.

"You don't know how I hate notoriety, and how alien it is to my nature!" And she sat down to write an answer to Dr. Webster, making the deepest apologies to the little doctor, because she was so fond of him, "But," she went on, "this is something that I cannot do. I would feel like a curiosity or a freak to these prying people, and above all else I want to do my work without notice."

An hour later the reply came. The little professor, who had been insistent before, answered now in quite another mood. "I understand your feelings perfectly, and I honor them."

"Do you see, Henry! Do you see what a splendid person he can be!"

She began eagerly to dress herself. It had been arranged that she was to go quietly with her brother, to the Presbyterian Church where the exercises were to be held, and there they would wait, quite unrecognized, until the procession should arrive.

Miss Waller, who had come up to help Elizabeth with

her costume, chased Henry from the room. "Get off with you," she cried, "and be presentable for this grand occasion."

"And you," she said to Elizabeth, as she hooked her into the somber black dress that the latter had chosen, "I swear I've dressed many a bride, but I've never seen anyone half so nervous."

Elizabeth looked around, and her face, always thoughtful, was radiant. "It's a strange thing," she said, "but I *feel* like a bride. I feel . . . I feel that my life's just beginning."

And she fastened at her throat the silver brooch her mother had sent her, and smoothed down the heavy gown which the little orphan girl at Blockley had so much admired.

Walking to the church with her brother, she was silent, and he also did not speak. When they saw the crowd outside, he was, however, at once the man of action. Calling out an usher, he got a key and let Elizabeth in through a side door, where an empty pew well to the front was pointed out to them. There they sat down unrecognized although there was some craning of necks from the balconies where the ladies were seated.

Then as the organist took his place and struck up the processional air, all heads turned toward the doors, where the graduates headed by the Bishop of New York in his gown, and the president of the college in full academic dress, were entering.

Solemnly, to the sound of music, the procession marched down the central aisle and toward the platform. As the last student in the line of march reached Elizabeth, he stopped and offered her his arm.

She stood up, stepped into the aisle, and aware suddenly of a silence and the feeling of all eyes upon her, she placed her fingers on his arm, and in her swaying gown, and to the sound of the music she marched past the crowded pews to the front row of seats where she took her place with the other students.

Dr. Benjamin Hale, looking more birdlike than ever with a small tuft of black hair standing up in front of his academic cap, began at once to confer the diplomas. He called up four students at a time, and his voice ringing out in sonorous Latin, quickly passed over their names. *Domine* Smith, *domine* Fields . . . the academic titles seemed strange but full of dignity.

Elizabeth waited, feeling weak, hot and cold by turns. Pressing her fingers together, she tried desperately to control herself.

She was called up last. The president, who had not removed his scholastic hat for the others, now did so. He addressed her likewise in Latin, but pausing so that everyone could hear, he substituted the feminine word *domina* for the masculine word he had used with the others.

Elizabeth bowed, took the diploma, half turned to go, and then as if the full significance of the moment had burst on her, she heard herself speaking.

"Sir, I thank you. . . ." She hesitated. "By the help of the Most High it shall be the effort of my life to shed honor upon your diploma!"

Three months later she left for Paris to undertake the study of surgery. She had no notion whether the French hospitals would admit her.

CHAPTER SEVEN

*B*UT ELIZABETH, HOW CAN YOU *DO* IT!"

It was Anna who was speaking, and in her agitation she
had opened the French doors of their little apartment on the
pleasant Rue de Fleurus, and looking out for a moment, she
frowned down on the Luxembourg Garden with its tiny
rimmed lake and clipped trees, as though even this view
were annoying to her.

She turned back to Elizabeth. "Do you really mean to
enter La Maternité?"

Elizabeth nodded.

"As a student apprentice!" Her sister was horrified. "To

carry trays and wash patients! And wear an apron and maybe even wooden *sabots* like any peasant girl!"

"Please, Anna . . ."

"I don't understand you, really I don't!" And for ten minutes with her full and vigorous use of language, Elizabeth's older sister did not stop speaking.

"You're a physician, are you not? . . . You have a diploma from a recognized American school . . ."

"Yes! Yes!" Elizabeth got up. "But don't you see there isn't a college, a hospital, a *clinique*, or a surgery in Paris that will recognize it. . . ."

And this was quite true. Elizabeth had been a month in Paris, having come, of course, with the hope of being admitted as a post-graduate student in surgery at one of the better Parisian hospitals. At every hospital she had been refused admission. It was inconceivable to the French directors that a woman could be a physician or that she could want such privileges. There was nothing in their rules to provide for it. They shrugged their shoulders and turned away. Even when the American consul interceded for her, the impression was still the same. Either the young American lady was insane, or very nearly so, and to calm her they treated her with exaggerated but firm politeness.

After a month of this treatment, Elizabeth decided to enter the big woman's hospital, La Maternité, as a common nursing apprentice. She couldn't conceive of going back to America without at least seeing the inside of one of these great institutions about which she had heard so much. But Anna, when she heard of this decision, was horrified.

"What about Professor Louis?" she asked again desperately. "Can't he do anything?"

"Nothing! Nothing at all!" replied Elizabeth. "Professor Pierre Charles Alexander Louis may be the most famous surgeon in France, but even he can't help me."

"I know. . . ." Anna burst out. "But what actually did he say?"

"He advises me most strongly to enter La Maternité."

"As an ignorant, untrained three-month student. Like some peasant girl from the provinces or some silly little *grisette!*"

"What you don't see," replied Elizabeth, "is that I will be living in one of the oldest and finest hospital on the Continent . . . with thousands of specialized cases . . . the greatest surgeons in attendance . . . the most modern techniques." She turned to her sister, and her manner was no longer calm. In fact, Anna had never seen her display such feeling, for usually Elizabeth was quite composed.

"What does it matter that I will make beds and will wash babies?" she said. "I will still have my eyes to see, won't I!" And she turned away from her sister.

Anna did not speak for a moment. And beginning in her nervous way to straighten out some papers which lay on the table, she stopped, shook her head and turned to Elizabeth.

"It may be," she said, "that you are a great woman." She smiled. "But it's very hard to see such things in one's family."

The next morning the two sisters got up early and drove to the hospital which lay near the Pantheon in another and older quarter of the city.

Once a convent, the hospital had retained much of its medieval character: high walls above which slanted towers showed, and inside innumerable courtyards surrounded by *cloîtres,* the convenient arched passages which connected the labyrinthine corridors of the old buildings.

In the first courtyard a great crowd of chattering girls were gathered. "Leave me here," said Elizabeth. "I shall write you when to come."

And she took her place at the end of a long weaving line of young women, surging forward toward a small door with a wicket, and a red-faced old woman in a tremendous cap who was calling out names very impatiently.

Some of the girls in the courtyard were peasants, as Elizabeth could tell from their high, starched headdresses trimmed with ribbons, and their wide colorful skirts carefully pleated after the manner of their individual provinces. Some in the wide gowns and the feathered little bonnets of the Parisian grisettes were of a different type altogether, far more self-possessed and sophisticated. Very curiously they looked at Elizabeth in her plain gray dress and gray bonnet.

When Elizabeth was called up, she showed her birth certificate, her passport, and the mark on her arm of the recent vaccination she had been warned would be necessary.

All were approved and she passed into a long room lined with benches, where there was more waiting, more questions. It was dark before all the details of her admission were settled, and she was sent with fifteen other girls to the *dortoir* assigned them, a long student dormitory in the infirmary quarters.

The room, which was low, immense, and divided in the center by an arched doorway, was lined from end to end by rows of small iron cots, separated by white curtains.

Elizabeth's trunk was brought up and a little lamp was placed on the table. She was at once starting to undress, when the girl from the next cot lifted the curtains and looking up in a very forlorn and homesick manner began to talk in a peculiar French dialect.

At first Elizabeth could not understand what she was saying. But finally it was clear to her. The girl was introducing herself.

"I am Marie Josette," she was saying. "My father is a farmer in the mountains near the town of Bescançon," and she began to ask Elizabeth about herself.

She surveyed Elizabeth with frank curiosity. "Are you from England?" she asked.

"I am an American," said Elizabeth.

The little peasant girl was astonished. "But how can that be?" she said, sitting up and staring at Elizabeth. "Are not all Americans black?"

Elizabeth, tired as she was, could not help laughing. "Some are not," she said, and while she went on undressing, turning away from the girl, who had no notion of privacy, she explained where this strange land of America was located, how far away it was, and how long it had taken the ship to travel.

At all this her neighbor was amazed. Was not America an island? Was it not near Havana? And for some time her questions would not stop.

A week later Elizabeth sat on the edge of her bed one evening and by a very poor light was composing a letter to an English cousin whom she had visited before her arrival in Paris, and whom she had kept informed of her plans. "There are personal objections connected with this course that I was not prepared for," she admitted; "that is, a strict imprisonment, very poor lodging and food, some rather menial services, and the loss of three or four nights of sleep every week."

On her first evening in the hospital, Elizabeth was called for duty in the *salle d' accouchements* where the babies were born. This was a large upper room, dimly lighted, with beds all along the walls, a fire on the hearth, cupboards full of linen, and shelves of shining copper and tin utensils.

In the center of the room was a large wooden stand which had a small protective railing, or fence. Here the newborn babies, tightly swathed and ticketed, were deposited one after another, as they arrived during the night.

On this particular occasion, as if in honor of Elizabeth's service, a record was broken. Eight babies were born, and when the chief midwife made her appearance the next morning, the white cloth drawn up like a tent over the table was removed in triumph and the newcomers were shown off. All had wrinkled red faces and the unbelievably old look of the newborn. Each baby wore a coarse peaked cap, on the front of which was pinned a label, displaying its family name and sex, a black serge jacket with a white handkerchief folded over the chest and arms, and a small blanket tightly pinned round the lower part of the body.

"Very well behaved, very well behaved, indeed!" cried Madame Charrier, looking down at the newcomers, who for an instant lay quiet like so many red-visaged little mummies and then with a single outburst started crying.

It was seven o'clock. Elizabeth, excused with the other *élèves,* stumbled off wearily to bed, to be called only two hours later for ward duty, then a lecture, then evening service in the chapel.

For months at a time the girls in service at La Maternité were not allowed outside the walls. All they saw of Paris was the patch of sky above the courtyard. Their hours of work were very long, "almost," said Elizabeth, "beyond my powers of physical endurance." And the lack of sleep, due to night-duty and the noise in the dormitories during the daytime, kept Elizabeth in a constant stage of fatigue. But what was even more trying than the long hours and the hard work was the complete lack of privacy, to which Elizabeth found it very hard to accustom herself. Locked up with fifteen other girls in the dormitory, most of them talkative, full of high spirits, and very noisy, she was not alone for a moment, day or night.

Even the baths of the *élèves,* as the student nurses were called, were taken in concert, six girls being called up at a time to a vast room in which a half a dozen tubs stood in a double row exactly in the center of the steaming bath chamber. A concierge of the bath was in charge, a wrinkled, toothless, but incessantly talkative old woman who filled the tubs, handed out the rough sheets for drying, and kept up a truculent, irritated one-sided dialogue all the while.

"I try to imagine that her voice is only the bubbling of water that I hear," wrote Elizabeth humorously. "I shut my eyes, lie quietly for half an hour, and fancy that I am deliciously reposing on the heaving waters of some soft summer lake. Then I spring up, take a cold dash, to the horror of my companions, and hurry off as fast as possible."

In the dormitory, even if she had a few minutes after her bath, it was quite impossible to rest. Some of the girls who had been up during the night in the infirmary might be sleeping, but that seemed no reason at all why the others should keep quiet. They came banging in and out continually, sat on their beds, eating, or talking and laughing, if not making a much greater noise. Sometimes there were pillow fights, or else in the height of excitement they set the beds "promenading."

The bedsteads, made of iron, were placed on rollers so movable that the slightest touch would set them rolling. It was a favorite sport among some of the girls to place a bedstead at the end of the room and drive it with great violence down the center. The rolling noise over the brick floor was tremendous. Some of the girls would get on top of the bed, others would push it, and a whole row of beds would be set promenading.

On such occasions it was not long before Madame Blockel, the superintendent of the *dortoirs*, came rushing in. A small, thin woman with a reddish nose and big protruding teeth, she would burst in at least once a day, accuse somebody or other, and raising her voice would scream herself hoarse in a voluble French that even Elizabeth with her knowledge of this language could not follow. Very often the girls would scream back. Everybody would get out of bed and take excited part in the quarrel which would usually die down as suddenly as it had started.

The first time this happened, Elizabeth was shocked and very much disturbed. But before long she became accustomed to these unaccountable storms and could continue with her writing or resting as though nothing were happening.

"Morning, noon, and night," she wrote in her journal, "good Madame Blockel's voice drowns all opposing sounds; and really now I am getting as used to it as to a noisy street,

and would not care if only she would keep out of the *dortoir*
at night when I am sleepy, for like a barking dog, she sets
all the girls going, and I don't know when the storm sub-
sides, for I sink to sleep in spite of it."

Elizabeth was fortunate enough to have a window behind her bed, and by pushing the bedstead forward she had
managed to fit in a chair behind. With her dressing gown
hung up on the curtain rod, and her books arranged on the
floor beside her, she would retire to this cubby hole, where
despite all the noise and confusion she would try in her odd
moments to write and study. But usually, as soon as she sat
down, a tingling, intoxicating sense of weariness would
come over her, and frequently, sitting by the window, she
would fall asleep.

The routine of the hospital was incessant, the hours of
work tremendous. At half past five in the morning the girls
were out of their beds, and behind their chief, one Madame
Madeline Edmée Clementine (Huscherard) Charrier, were
on their way to the wards.

Elizabeth hastened upstairs to the long corridor, the
Sainte-Elizabeth, for which she was responsible. It was her
duty, every morning, to wash the patients in her charge, see
to their beds, and make inquiries as to their condition. In a
big coarse white apron tied over her morning gown, Elizabeth bustled about the ward, and straightening the beds, she
spoke in her halting French with each patient.

"*Mademoiselle l'anglaise,*" they called her, and whispered
from bed to bed that she was as good as a doctor, this pale,
foreign-looking young nurse who was always so serious and
so concerned and attentive when they described their troubles to her and spoke of their symptoms.

She was forever stopping at their beds and asking questions, and noting down many strange things in a little black
notebook that she carried.

"Do you mark us down for your prayers?" one sick woman
asked.

But Elizabeth did not have time to answer. She must go flying about the ward this morning with her big apron flapping, for in no time at all the chief *sage-femme*, keen-eyed Madame Charrier would be at the door. And Elizabeth, standing at attention in the doorway, would be accountable to her for the condition of the ward.

Madame Charrier was a slight, elderly woman, who had a habit of cocking her head sideways and speaking out sharply. But her eyes were blue, and her manner for all her sternness was not unfriendly. She had been in the hospital twelve years, and had the manner of a veteran, whom nothing could frighten and nothing amaze.

She could not quite make Elizabeth out. Why should such a ladylike and well-informed person subject herself to the drudgery of the big state hospital? And for some reason she was more sharp with her than with the others.

"The floor in the corner is dusty, mademoiselle."

"Yes, madame!"

"How many counterpanes have you called for this week?" she would ask, or else with a note of sharpness she would complain, "Ah, you English, how lavish you are with the soap!"

She could never remember Elizabeth's nationality. America was so far away, England nearby. How was it possible she had come so far? And what for? To make beds at La Maternité? It was all quite incomprehensible.

But sometimes, when in a more friendly mood, she would question Elizabeth about the patients under her care. And it was amazing. The girl knew, she confided to her assistant, Mlle. Mallet, more than any doctor.

"How is the one with the fever?" she would ask, "And the delicate one in the corner, has she begun to eat again?"

For all her tremendous responsibilities, the old woman chief was capable of worrying about her patients, and accordingly came in time to rely on Elizabeth.

"I wish," she said one morning, "that all the wards were

so well attended. Ah, these girls," she exclaimed, "they are willing enough, but they have no understanding."

By seven o'clock in the morning the ward inspection was over. Elizabeth, hastening to the *dortoir* after an hour and a half on her feet without breakfast, would feel dizzy as she hurried to make up her bed and put her cubby in order. And then with a little white pot in her hand, she would cross the courtyard to the window of the infirmary where morning coffee was sold to the girls for two sous a dipper. The day before, the morning bread had been given out, a long thin crusty loaf which she kept in a napkin under her pillow. Then swinging her feet slightly under her long skirt, for the bed was the most comfortable place to sit on, she would break off the bread and, like the French girls around her, would dip it, unbuttered, into her coffee, which was hot, bitter with chicory and colored a dull gray with milk.

The last part of the breakfast was always hurried, because at eight the visits of the attending physicians would begin, and this was the high event of the day for all who worked in the wards. The *élèves*, standing at attention until they entered, followed the doctors from bed to bed, discreetly. Sometimes a case was explained, sometimes orders were given briefly.

This was a nervous hour for everyone but Elizabeth, who looked forward the whole day to this event, drinking in every word that was spoken, and trying to restrain herself from the inevitable questions that rose to her lips.

M. Louis Girardin, the chief physician, was a tall, gray-haired man with a full shining beard which he stroked sideways, parting it nervously as he stood over his patients. Everybody stood in great awe of him, even Madame Charrier, who noted every word that he said, and then repeated it. But it was to the young interne, M. Blot, that Elizabeth's attention was for some reason drawn. Tall, quiet, with eyes somewhat like those of Dr. Benedict, whom she had so much admired at Blockley, he could be distinguished, withdrawn, and yet unspeakably gentle—especially where the patients were concerned.

With the young women *élèves*, however, he was exceedingly formal, almost shy. Elizabeth he treated very coldly, as though he feared her, and for some reason was embarrassed in her presence.

One morning when Elizaebth was on duty in the ward alone, he came in, and stopping at the bed where she was attending a sick woman, he put some questions to her.

She answered so intelligently, showed such a complete and comprehensive knowledge of the woman's condition, that he was surprised and, walking to the doorway with her, he said, "You know a great deal more than the others."

Elizabeth did not immediately confide her background, but was pleased that he had recognized it. The next time he saw her in the wards, he told her of a medical journal which described just the case about which they had been talking. Then, forgetting himself, he offered to loan the journal to her.

For the first time since coming to La Maternité, she was encouraged, for the work, she had to admit to herself, had been menial and trying. And sometimes when she was very tired and discouraged, she had felt like leaving, like giving up altogether. It was so hard to conceal what she was, so hard to pretend that she knew almost nothing. Now to talk to M. Hippolyte Blot, who was intelligent and well informed, gave her a sense of standing up, of drawing a full breath at last, after a long period of being cramped and constricted.

Learning by rote was the method of instruction for the students, who gathered under the shade of a big tree in the ancient wood behind the hospital, when the weather was warm. Each group of new students was assigned to an older and more experienced one. The young teacher, herself not too well informed, would hold up a *papier-mâché* duplicate of some part of the skelton, perhaps the arm, and pointing out the ulna bone or the radius, would pass this object around, asking each girl to repeat the name after her.

But even this learning by repetition was difficult for them, and Elizabeth always took the precaution of hesitating when it came to her turn. She did not want to appear too glib before the others.

One day, the *ancienne élève*, as the student teacher was called, became confused. "The blood," she said, "the blood . . ." And she began to rummage for the right place in her book but could not find it.

Elizabeth, who could not help herself, said quickly that she was prepared in just this part of the lesson. And offering to recite, she was soon launched on a careful, clear explanation of the theory of blood circulation.

The chief of the group stopped rummaging in her book; the girls in the group sat at attention; and soon some other *élèves* from other groups stopped and also remained to listen.

Elizabeth, aware of their attention, stopped suddenly. But the leader of the group, who was a frank and simple-hearted girl and very conscientious about teaching her charges, interrupted her. "Please," she said, "go on. You can do it so much better than I."

After that she not only asked Elizabeth to recite at length when difficult points were to be covered in the lesson, but came to her frequently herself, to ask for explanations on the advanced work she was studying. What happened soon after that was that mysteriously it became known in all the *dortoirs* that *Mademoiselle l'anglaise* was unfathomable in her knowledge, and wherever Elizabeth appeared, the girls who were vexed with their lessons came to her for help.

"By the Virgin," said one simple girl, crossing herself, "there is nothing which she does not know." She even asked for advice about her *beaux*, wishing to know if Elizabeth could phrenologize her, and could tell by the bumps on her head what she ought to do.

Elizabeth sighed. "I do not know what to do myself, sometimes!"

"That is impossible," said the simple *élève*, whom Elizabeth had nicknamed La Normandy, because it happened she came from this province.

But in spite of this admission, Elizabeth's reputation grew, and even Madame Charrier came in time to depend on her, as did all the other teachers in the infirmary. Every morning, after the student session had begun, Madame Charrier would examine the students for an hour. On these occasions it was her habit to have Elizabeth beside her, and if a student faltered, she would say, turning the offender over to her, "If you cannot pound something into that dull head, then by the Saints, it cannot be done."

Madame Charrier took her teaching very seriously, and noted with satisfaction Elizabeth's natural abilities in this direction. If a girl answered promptly and well, at the morning examination, her satisfaction would be extreme, and her face would grow beautiful. "*Bien! très bien!*" she would say, as though the greatest miracle had been accomplished. But if a girl faltered, became confused, and as some did, started to cry, she would be beside herself.

She would rise from her chair, clap her hands together with the greatest vehemence, shake her body from side to side, and looking up to heaven as if to ask why such a misfortune should be visited on her, she would say to all that her life was a failure, and she was certainly, most certainly giving up the effort to teach anyone! However, if in the midst of this agitated recitative the offending student managed somehow to blurt out the answer, "*Ah bien! très bien!*" all was forgotten and student and teacher were locked in each other's arms.

Elizabeth could never get over her wonder at this performance, and her greater wonder still at the strength and vitality of the old woman, who, though seemingly delicate, could go through several such scenes a day.

Sometimes if a student was particularly and unpardon-
ably stupid, she would take quite another attack. Folding
her hands in a gesture of utter and complete resignation, she
would ask quietly from which province or department the
student had come.

When the mumbled answer was given, a province near
Marseille, or the fourteenth *arrondissement* in Paris, however the case might be, she would sigh deeply, shake her
head profoundly, and say with a gesture of deep hopelessness and the most biting sarcasm, "Ah, then it is all account-
ed for. No wonder, mademoiselle, that your case is quite
without hope."

This remark always brought on tears, and afterwards the
discouraged *élève* would seek out Elizabeth in the corridor,
or in her cubby. "Ah, mademoiselle, what would we do
without you! You heard . . . you heard what she said, my
case is quite without hope."

Then more tears, until Elizabeth would explain the lesson. After that there would be a present under Elizabeth's
pillow, a bit of cheese sent from the country by the girl's
mother, or one of those paper-covered cups of *chocolat
mousse* which were forever being smuggled into the infirmary from the *pâtisserie* outside, and which were considered by the girls to be the greatest of delicacies.

The patients whom Elizabeth attended also showed their
gratitude. Elizabeth was very much moved to receive, one
day, a *prie-dieu,* a little prayer trinket which a very sick
woman had made for her. "I shall pray for you always,
mademoiselle," she said, and pressed the religious symbol
into her hand.

Elizabeth put the *prie-dieu* into her Bible, where she was
to find it many years later, carefully folded between the
pages. And, looking back, she was to think of her period of
service at the French hospital as one of the most profitable
periods in her whole career as a student.

But most of the time she was too rushed and too hurried

to do any thinking. Every hour, every minute of the day, it seemed, was apportioned, and there was never time to do all that had to be done, or feel all that was passing.

Every day had a function. Monday was linen day, Tuesday was vaccination day. Promptly at one o'clock the new babies were rolled into the hall of nurses.

In the center of the room sat M. Blot, and because Elizabeth was far more deft than any of the other *élèves*, she was always placed in a chair nearby. As each child was handed to her, she would quickly uncover the baby's arm, and the interne would touch it with a small knife moistened in the precious vaccine.

Sometimes Elizabeth would address a question. Where M. Blot had formerly been shy, almost cold, he was now friendly. Instead of passing his hand through his hair and looking intently at the baby as though he had never seen an infant before, he would smile, answer with interest, and even offer interesting comments.

One afternoon when it was quite sunny in the ward, and he knew that Elizabeth would be *en service* there, he brought down his microscope of which he was exceedingly proud. He put the instrument on a window ledge in the corner of the room and, sitting down, allowed Elizabeth to peer through the glass while he adjusted the slides.

He had brought down some tiny fragments of skin to show her, and he explained the formation of the round and the elongated cells. Then he pricked his finger and, drawing a tiny globule of blood, allowed her to view it under the microscope.

He let her adjust and focus the microscope, and told her how to prepare the slides. When she had to go away to a patient, he asked her if she wouldn't return, as he had something interesting to tell her. When she came back, he confided that he had made some original researches and was hoping at the interne's examination to do well enough so that he might stand a chance for the gold medal.

"You cannot imagine, mademoiselle," he said, "what it will mean to me. It will open all doors. . . ."

And Elizabeth smiled almost bitterly, looked down at her coarse apron and work-reddened hands. Why should it be so hard for her, and only for one reason? But a moment later she caught herself. She had never allowed herself such thoughts. Taking M. Blot's hand, she gave him her good wishes and told him she was certain of his success.

The next day he mentioned a friend, Claude Bernard, a student of physiology, "whose experiments," he said, "will remake the whole world of medicine!" He would have told her more, would have explained the nature of these experiments, but again a patient called her, and again she had to rush away, for day and night the heavy duties of the ward never seemed to cease.

Yet in all this hard work, the sleepless nights, the long hours, there were moments of gratification. It was the custom for each student superior, and for the teachers as well, to have assistants present when they visited the patients at their bedsides. As questions were asked of the patient, as to background, his history, his present condition, it was the duty of the assistant to write down the answers, as she heard them. It was also her duty to take dictation from the chief, who composed a résumé of the case at the bedside.

One day Elizabeth was taking this dictation from Mlle. Mallet, one of the teachers. But when the latter was through, Elizabeth, who had observed the patient very closely, felt there were certain important points that had not been covered. She could not help adding to what had been dictated. Then she handed all the material in, together.

The case history, like all the others, was reviewed by Madame Charrier, who immediately called her subordinate in to congratulate her.

But, said Mlle. Mallet, "these are not my observations. I did not write them." A moment later she remembered and volunteered the information that it must have been Mademoiselle Blackwell, her assistant, who had composed the material.

Elizabeth was called in, and stood very quiet, expecting a reproof. Instead, both women got up, and with the French emotion which is always free and direct, they shook her hand, and congratulated her.

"*Bon! Bon!*" clucked Madame Charrier, who had for some-time been observing Elizabeth. "You not only have hands, you have a head!"

A short time later, the *directeur* of the school, M. Paul Antoine Dubois, stopped Elizabeth in the hallway one morning, and suggested that she go on for the full two-year course, instead of the three-month semester for which she had been admitted.

"We feel certain," he said, "that you would be one of our most notable graduates."

"But I am already a graduate of an American school, a full school of medicine," she insisted.

M. Dubois waved his hands. "Ah," he said, "but there is only one La Maternité!"

The diploma she had shown him on entering, he had hardly considered. Being a woman, she could obviously not be a physician, so obviously this document for all its pretensions must be worthless. But he was willing to admit and so did the other surgeons that she had very unusual talents, and might some day make an excellent *sage-femme* if she completed the full course of training open to women.

As for her great interest in surgery, it was really pathetic. Had she been a man, then of course her ambitions could have been encouraged. However, as a special concession, it was granted that she might attend operations whenever they occurred.

Late one night, during a terrific rainstorm, Elizabeth awoke to find a candle held over her face and one of the *élèves* shaking her. There was to be a very rare emergency operation. Would she care to go at once to witness it?

Still sleepy, Elizabeth wound her hair up into a knob, pinned it securely, pulled a gown over her nightclothes, and hastily tying on her boots, ran down the long corridor toward the amphitheatre.

In the instance of a rare operation, students from all parts of Paris would come rushing in cabs. And Elizabeth, standing on her seat to see better, was the only woman present.

The rain beat in torrents on the skylight, the wind shook the building, and the lamps which the internes held over the surgeon's head seemed to flicker and every moment threatened to go out. The patient had been given spirits of ether, inhaling it deeply from a moistened handkerchief held over his nostrils. The surgeon and his assistants worked in complete silence, except for a terse murmur when sponges were handed, or instruments were taken away.

Elizabeth, completely calm, felt only one longing, to hold the instruments herself, to feel that on her skill and on her knowledge the life of a human being could depend.

"But when will that be?" she thought bitterly, and lying in her bed later, could not sleep.

Still, for all her discouragement, she had decided to remain at the hospital a few months longer, for as M. Blot had pointed out, here in six months she might see more cases than the average physician would encounter in a lifetime.

When she had been in residence for four months, her first day of leave was allowed her. Her sister had to call for and promise to return her, just as for any naïve peasant girl who could not be trusted alone outside the gates of the hospital.

How gay and free and delightful the city seemed! She walked with Anna along the river, sauntered through the Tuileries. Then, taking a cab, they got off at the Luxembourg Gardens, where Elizabeth said she would like to sit for an hour in the sunshine.

"Just think," she said, "the whole summer is over." And

they watched the children playing in the piles of dead autumn leaves.

"Do you know," said Elizabeth, as she reviewed for her sister some of the happenings at the hospital, "with all the hardships, I would not part with the experience I've had."

Anna was about to say something, but her sister interrupted her. "For one thing," she went on, "it is now perfectly clear to me just what I must do. Somehow, some way I must accomplish it. I want more than anything else to become greatly skilled as a surgeon.

"This ambition has become so important to me . . ." She broke off, was silent, but at last went on to tell Anna that for the first time in her life she was not hopeful, was troubled in fact, by a strange kind of fear, a fear that she couldn't quite analyze. "Like something hanging over me. Pure nerves, of course. I would laugh it away in one of my patients."

"You're overworked," said Anna, "anyone can see that!"

At eight o'clock they were back, and Elizabeth, signing in at the window to the wizened, grumbling *Madame de Bureau,* turned to her sister.

"What I need is a rest," she said. "When this is all over we will travel through to the Continent. One of the girls read my fortune the other day and said, darkness and then a journey. Perhaps we will go through a tunnel. I can't give it any other interpretation." After the day's rest she felt more cheerful than she had for several weeks.

Several weeks later, Elizabeth was on service in the infirmary, when a slight accident happened. Called down very early to take care of a baby whose eyes were infected, she took up the sick child sleepily. In the early morning dark and also because she was tired, she did not handle the eye syringe with skill, for she was aware as she bent over the infant, that a little of the liquid had spurted into her own eye.

During the day it felt to her as though there were a little

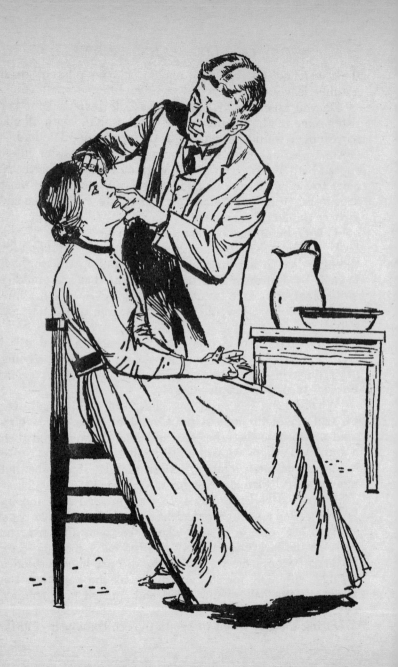

grain of sand under her lid. She was afraid to think what it might be, for the child had been afflicted with ophthalmia, the infectious eye disease which destroys the sight of so many children.

"It's nothing," she said to herself, "absolutely nothing!" and refused to look in the mirror or examine herself.

But by night the eye was swollen, and in the morning she could not open it. Holding a handkerchief to her eye, she went at once to the infirmary, where the shocked and solicitous face of the surgeon told her the verdict.

A bed was made for her at once in the infirmary. Her sister was sent for. And M. Blot, hearing what had happened, asked the chief surgeon if he might be relieved of all other duties for a few days, so that he could personally superintend her care.

The infection spread through the whole body, and alternately she trembled, or else felt as if her face, her skin, the whole bed were on fire. The pain in her eye and head was continual.

Hour by hour, through the days and through the nights the treatments continued, cold compresses to the head, leeches to the temple, ointment of belladonna to the eyes, and opium to the forehead.

Sometimes she was feverish and in her delirium was aware that she did not know what she was saying. Once she awoke in the gray light of early morning or else of twilight, she could not tell which, and looking up was aware of a shadowy, wavering figure by her bedside. It was M. Blot.

She tried to smile. "When did you come?" she asked.

"*Sh-h,*" he motioned that she must be quiet. "I have not been away."

Sometimes Anna sat by her bed, and sometimes Madame Charrier herself, who was deeply concerned. As for Mlle. Mallet, her former chief, she was at the beside constantly.

But Elizabeth, for whom the slightest movement was agonizing, lay with her eyes shut, either sleeping, trying to sleep, or else summoning her sources of strength for some kind of crisis she felt that she had to face, but which she was putting off, hour by hour.

Then one morning, the pain vanished. Her head was quite clear. She opened her eyes, but it seemed to her that even as she looked up the room grew dark, and the objects before her vision seemed to fade away.

"What's happening?" she cried. "I can't see!"

The chief surgeon was sent for and came immediately. With an exquisite delicacy of touch he removed from her affected eye the film that had formed over the pupil. For a moment Elizabeth saw his face clearly, and the face of M. Blot, standing just behind him, then as suddenly as if a curtain had been drawn, she was left in complete darkness.

The vision of the affected eye had been completely destroyed, and the other eye was so much impaired that it would be weeks before she would be able to see with it.

She lay listlessly in bed. What was there to get well for, what to get up for? A phrase of Dr. Webster's kept running in her mind, "blind hands . . . blind hands . . ." and she pressed her palms together to keep from screaming.

But finally even this mood passed. One day when she was feeling better, she asked the *élève* to bring her a comb, and carefully she combed out her hair which was long, light in color, and wavy. When M. Blot came in, she was braiding it.

"What beautiful hair!" he said, and he touched the long smooth braid with his fingers.

Then he began to talk to her about the Protestant religion. "If I ever changed from the church in which I have always worshipped," he said, "I know that no other belief would appeal to me as much as yours."

When Elizabeth was better and able to be up for a little while each day, she discussed with Mlle. Mallet the kind of present which "a grateful patient might give to her physician."

Mlle. Mallet smiled. "M. Blot?" she said.

Elizabeth nodded. "Would you buy for me an elegant pair of lamps for his consultation rooms?"

Elizabeth could now see a little, and at Anna's request had decided to leave the hospital, since it had been suggested she might recover more quickly in the country or at some watering place.

On the evening before the departure the lamps arrived, and were stowed away in Mlle. Mallet's room, lest M. Blot should happen to come in and see them before, as Elizabeth said, "it was time for the unveiling."

Wrapped in a dressing gown and shawl, and looking and feeling very much like a ghost, Elizabeth hurried through the corridors, to see the gift. The lamps, at her request, were to be conveyed to his rooms that night.

The next morning he came to thank her. "I will never forget, mademoiselle," he said, "never."

Elizabeth took his hand. "I wish you," she said, "all happiness."

The morning had been full of excitements, all the *élèves* from her *dortoir*, and many others coming to say good-bye. Madame Charrier neglected her early rounds and came twice, both times with last-minute directions for Elizabeth's care. And finally came the *directeur*, M. Dubois, for a dignified visit.

He had not known, he said, had not fully realized the extent of Elizabeth's talents. When she was better, when her eyes were fully recovered, and she returned to Paris to study, he himself would get entree for her to the very best hospitals and *cliniques*.

All this Elizabeth told to M. Blot, and he stood listening. "I will get well," she said. "I will do what I planned. My whole life is pointed in that direction."

He sighed. "I wish you all success, mademoiselle," he said. "But you have chosen a hard way, a very hard way for a woman."

An hour later, bandaged and veiled, she was ready to go.

The carriage drove to the door, Anna guided her in. Elizabeth sank back in the seat, said nothing. But later, in Anna's rooms, she laughed hysterically the whole evening.

For some months after that, while Elizabeth sought a cure at the famous hospitals and watering places of Europe, the subject of surgery was not mentioned between the two sisters. And for some reason, the name of the young interne who had been so kind to Elizabeth did not come up in the conversation either.

When she returned to Paris in May, almost exactly a year after her coming, she was filled out, seemed more serious, looked older. The sight of one eye was irreparably gone, the other one would never be too efficient. To think of surgery as a profession was out of the question.

But from St. Bartholomew's Hospital in London, where some friends had interceded for her, had come a cordial invitation. The dean of the hospital, famous Professor James Paget himself, assured her that she would be welcome as a graduate student. The ticket of admission was enclosed. . . .

In England she was greeted like a heroine, was entertained at breakfast by the famous Dr. Paget, in his home on the hospital grounds, had so many invitations to parties that she had to refuse them. Besides her studies, which took her to most of the hospitals of London, she made several very interesting friendships.

There was dark-haired, delicate Florence Nightingale, who talked of one subject incessantly, the need of good women to train themselves as nurses. They had become friends immediately, and one day in the spring when they had been walking together at Embley Park, the fine country home of the Nightingales, the young Englishwoman drew Elizabeth's attention to the handsome building which stood on the grounds.

"Do you know what I always think when I look at that row of windows?" she said.

Elizabeth looked at her. She had never seen such fervor, such intensity. And yet her friend was so often ill, seemed actually to have no strength at all, except for a kind of spiritual glow that seemed to fill her body.

"What would you do?" said Elizabeth.

Miss Nightingale turned to her. "I think," she said, "how I should turn that great room into a hospital ward."

And walking along with Elizabeth, she explained how she might place the beds, and how she would organize the work of such a hospital.

As they were about to part, the young Englishwoman put out her hand. "Do you know," she said, "I would be perfectly happy working with you."

With Lady Byron, the widow of the poet, Elizabeth also made friends. A slender little old woman, inexpressibly dainty, Lady Byron had interested herself in the most serious of movements, and when she heard of Elizabeth's presence in England, she invited her for a visit in her large old stone house near Brighton.

They discussed medicine and also the growing movement of women's rights. In Worcester, Massachusetts, a "Woman's Rights Convention" had been held.

"But I cannot sympathize fully with an anti-man movement," said Elizabeth. "I have had too much kindness, aid, and just recognition from men to make such an attitude of women otherwise than painful."

Elizabeth was aware that Miss Stone, of whom her brother Henry was so fond, was a very strong worker in this movement. And Henry too was leaning more and more towards participation, her mother had written her.

Elizabeth's decision was to return to America. July 26, 1851, the date was inscribed on her passport. It was two years since she had been home!

CHAPTER EIGHT

*H*OW," SAID ELIZABETH, "CAN I RENT THE ROOM if you will not let me put out a sign? It's a doctor's suite, isn't it? That's how you advertised it!"

"Yes," said the landlady, "that's how I advertised it!"

"Then if I pay the rent, am I not entitled to the privileges . . ."

For a full half hour Elizabeth had been arguing with the landlady about the use of her front parlor as an office, and always they came back to the same point, that Elizabeth was a woman and women could not be physicians.

"But I am a physician," said Elizabeth. "I am a physician, duly graduated from an accredited school, duly registered by the state medical board, fully qualified in every way to carry on my work."

"All the same," said the landlady, "you may not put a sign on my premises!"

With this Elizabeth, who for more than three weeks had been searching for professional lodgings in New York, had to be satisfied. Everywhere else she had been looked upon with amazement as a quack, as a swindler, as some kind of monstrosity. Real estate agents had refused to deal with her, and landlords had been scandalized at the idea of renting to a woman physician. So to be received at all, she reflected after she had transported her things and had looked around at her surroundings, was in a way an accomplishment.

The room was high, a "stoop" parlor, in a red brick house at 44 University Place, once genteel, now looking out rather shabbily on the green open space of Washington Square. A good location, not at all unsuitable, but how was anyone to guess that behind the dusty curtains of the front parlor there was a physician waiting to practice?

With envy, Elizabeth noticed the sign of another doctor in a window down the street, but had to be contented with hanging up her diploma over her desk, polishing her instruments, and waiting not too nervously for patients.

It was hot, late August, and for two weeks she waited, watching the people go by her window, and feeling lonely, lost and fatigued in the heat and the haze of the city. Sometimes when it was cooler in the evening she walked out. Sometimes, taking a horsecar, she would ride along Broadway to the Croton Reservoir. There, far uptown, near Fortieth Street, where the houses were set far apart and trees shaded the roadway, there was a cottage restaurant which was much attended by ladies with their escorts, who rode out in the cool air to be served ice cream and other light refreshments, on the gay white verandah. But of course, Elizabeth, being alone, did not go up. It was enough of a venture that she had come so far unattended.

Sometimes she took the omnibus to the Battery and to Castle Garden, where, once or twice, she stood up with the others at the edge of the great reverberating banner-draped hall, waved her handkerchief when the lady singer came out on the platform, and listened to the opera airs and the military marches always played at the big free summer concerts.

But more frequently she kept to her room, planning, thinking, devising some means to make herself known in the city. Dr. Warrington had sent her some letters to some Quaker friends of his, but it was too early in the season to call. Besides, they would think much more of her if she had accomplished something for herself before she appeared.

On the first cool morning, she put on a black gown, her most dignified dress, an English bonnet, and taking with her a notice she had written out carefully the evening before, she went to call on Mr. Horace Greeley, the editor of New York's most important paper, the *Tribune*.

As it happened, just as she entered, Mr. Greeley himself came into the outer room with some papers in his hand for a messenger. Elizabeth, recognizing him from a picture she had seen, went up to him.

"Mr. Greeley," she said, "I have come to find out how liberal you are."

He turned around, his black eyes snapping. "Who are you, in heaven's name? What do you want?"

"I am Dr. Elizabeth Blackwell," she said.

The look of irritation vanished. He laughed, put out his hand. "Then you're Anna Blackwell's sister! She's a fine journalist . . ."

"She's *my* sister!" said Elizabeth.

He laughed again.

The next day the item which Elizabeth had prepared appeared word for word in the *Tribune*. "Miss Elizabeth Blackwell, M.D., has returned to this city from a two years' residence abroad, which she spent at the hospital of La Maternité in Paris, and at St. Bartholomew's Hospital in London. She has just opened an office at Number 44, University Place, and is prepared to practice in every department of her profession."

The notice was better than an advertisement, for Mr. Greeley's paper was read like a Bible both in anti-slave and in all liberal circles. Within a week Elizabeth had three letters from ladies asking her to make professional visits. She went, received her fee and was recommended to other patients.

One of these, an old Quaker woman, very sick with pneumonia, caused Elizabeth some concern. Young Dr. Blackwell told the old lady's relatives that while she was certain the patient would recover, the illness was grave, and they could if they wished have a consultation of physicians. They replied that any consultant whom Elizabeth called would be agreeable.

She knew no one in New York upon whom she could rely professionally, or who would respond on being invited by a woman physician. Then she happened to remember that the doctor who had treated her father in his last illness was now living in the city, and at once she sent off a note to him.

He came to the home of the sick woman, as she had requested, went up with Elizabeth to examine her, and then came down again. Elizabeth, following him a moment later, came into the parlor, where he was walking up and down nervously, his hands under his coat tail, his head bent forward as if in great agitation.

"A most extraordinary case!" he said, turning to her. "Such a one as has never happened to me before." He put his hand to his beard, pulled at it perplexedly. "I really do not know what to do!" he exclaimed.

She looked at him in amazement. "Why it's a clear case of pneumonia," she said, "and of no unusual danger!"

"Yes, yes, of course!" It seemed that it was not the case

that was troubling him at all. "It's the propriety," he burst out, "of consulting with a lady physician!"

Elizabeth was too astounded to feel angry or insulted. Instead she smiled, and her eyes, when she spoke, twinkled.

"Well," she said, picking up his hat and his stick deferentially, "let's not think of this as a consultation at all. Maybe you've paid me only a friendly visit!"

And the next time she needed a consultant for a case, she worded her note differently. Could she intrude on the time of her friend for a chat on some matters that troubled her? She signed the note with her given name only, so that the good doctor might not be embarrassed by her professional title. But as he began to appreciate that she was competent in her work, for Elizabeth had an intuitive skill when it came to making a diagnosis, he took to addressing her as doctor, and came in time to look on her, despite her sex, as a fellow physician.

But it took a long time for Elizabeth to achieve this recognition from the first physician with whom she had worked professionally, and she could write with truth to Lady Byron, after her first year of practice in New York, "I stand really alone. I have no medical companionship."

When she applied one day to the director of a big dispensary, offering her services as a physician, she received a cold, blunt reply. "Found your own dispensary!"

"Indeed I will!" she snapped.

And from this moment of anger came a plan. She rented a hall, the Hope Chapel Lecture Room, in the basement building of a Sunday School, and announced in the papers a series of lectures to be given for ladies. She charged an admission fee of two dollars, and with the help of some Quaker friends she had made, Mr. Stacy B. Collins, the merchant, and his married daughter, Mrs. Cornelia B. Hussey, she managed to get together an audience of about twenty ladies, who come week after week to hear her.

Her talks were entitled, *The Laws of Life with Special*

Reference to the Physical Education of Girls, and the audience responded to her medical information with interest. In fact, one woman, Mrs. Bellows, the wife of a minister, thought the lectures ought to be printed, and she prevailed upon Mr. George Putnam, the publisher, to bring out a paper-bound brochure.

The little book found its way to England, was read by the great critic and writer, Mr. John Ruskin, who commended it. And one day Elizabeth, who had been pleased at this notice, received a still greater surprise, a letter of congratulations from the dean of Geneva College, Dr. Lee!

Only recently, Elizabeth had had some angry correspondence with this gentleman. When she had been graduated, she had taken it for granted that her sister Emily, who also wanted to study medicine, and who was ready now to begin her training, would of course be admitted without question.

She was amazed to have the faculty write her that, while her own record was excellent, they could not set a precedent in this case, and accordingly would have to refuse admission to her sister.

Elizabeth, on receiving this refusal, had been quite bitter. As a result, Emily, who was as determined as her sister had been before her, was obliged to go halfway across the country to Chicago. There for a year she was permitted to study at the new Rush Medical College. But when the Illinois Society of Medicine discovered that a woman had been admitted, resolutions of censure were brought against the college, and Emily was asked to leave.

Elizabeth finally secured her admission at the medical school of Western Reserve University in Cleveland. But the experience was very disagreeable to her and showed clearly the difficulties that women still had to face.

"The matter will not be resolved," she said to her Quaker friend, Mrs. Hussey, "until we found a medical school for women ourselves, and turn out students well-trained and completely fitted for this important work!"

It was true that in Philadelphia a small school had been opened for women students of medicine, and another one in Boston. But neither institution gave full, complete, or competent training.

To have a college was Elizabeth's dream. But even more important was a hospital in which women students might practice, and if not a hospital, at least a dispensary. In the Eleventh Ward, near the river, where poor immigrant families were crowded together in a neighborhood of slaughterhouses, pens, and overpowering stenches, where there existed entire buildings known as "fever nests," and there was no medical charity of any kind, Elizabeth had made up her mind to establish a charity office to which women and children could come, and from which she might go out in her leisure hours to visit and teach health to poor families.

The sum of fifty dollars was needed to rent a room in this neighborhood for a few months, and a few dollars would be necessary for medical supplies and simple furnishings, a table, a few chairs, some curtains, a sign on the door.

"Thy good work shall not be wasted," said Mr. Collins when he had heard of her plan, and he offered to make a contribution. But his daughter interrupted him.

"This," she said, "is a matter for the charitable spirit of women!"

She at once proceeded to call a meeting of ladies in her home, and, getting up, introduced Elizabeth as the speaker. Some of the faces were curious, some were indifferent, and some were critical. Elizabeth, standing up to speak, and facing the ladies who had put down their teacups and were staring at her and through her with looks of frankest appraisal, as though to ask, "what kind of a phenomenon is this?" felt that by some means, by some special appeal, she must win them.

Discarding the talk she had planned, she began to speak about her own profession and its fitness for women.

"There is no line of practical work," she said, "outside of

domestic life, which is so suited to women as the study and practice of medicine."

She paused, felt the surprise of her audience, and went on. "The true physician must possess the essential qualities of maternity—tenderness—sympathy—guardianship!"

She talked of the mercy of women. Of Mrs. Elizabeth Fry, a Quakeress of gentle birth, who had risked her life to ease the sufferings of women prisoners. She spoke of Prudence Crandall, who had sacrificed her home, burnt down by indignant neighbors, when she insisted on giving instruction to Negro children.

She went on to describe the wretchedness and the misery she had seen in some of her visits to poor patients, of the Eleventh Ward, poorest and most crowded in the city, and yet not served by a single medical charity.

"Only women will look into such matter," she cried, "will have the heart and the sympathy to do so!"

She talked of a dispensary, very small, very modest, run by women, served by women, operated for the benefit of women and children alone.

And the audience, responding to her appeal, an appeal suited to women, "planned" as Mrs. Hussey later said, "with a most masterly skill," now nodded their heads in full approval. The looks of hostility had vanished. All faces were sympathetic, and all purses opened. Before the afternoon was over, and by the time the last of the callers had left, enthusiastically shaking Elizabeth's hand, Cornelia could announce from the dining room, where among the tea things she was counting the contributions, that the sum of "fifty dollars had, thanks to the Lord, been raised!"

The following day, the two women went house hunting, and found on Seventh Street, near Tompkins Square, a small room with a street entrance, that Elizabeth said would be exactly suitable. As for the disreputable surroundings, the pile of rubbish in the yard, the door which hung on its hinges, "We must come to those that need us," said Elizabeth, "surely they won't seek us out!"

And in a few days' time, the rubbish was cleaned out, the door was mended, the little room was whitewashed, and the few, simple borrowed furnishings were put into place. Mrs. Hussey hemmed some curtains for the windows, and tacking some old sheets over a carpenter's frame, she made a homemade screen.

"There," she said, smoothing the white cover on the cot, and giving a final touch to the row of medicines on the shelf, "The New York Dispensary for Indigent Women and Children is open! Let this be an auspicious beginning . . ."

The dispensary was to be open three days a week, on Monday, Wednesday, and Friday afternoons from three until six. And for an entire week, Elizabeth, sitting at her table, placed squarely near the window, waited for patients. None came.

Finally she threw the door open and sat in full view of those that passed. Children peered in, a woman, hurrying by with a bundle, looked up at the hand-lettered sign. A rheumatic old woman, shuffling painfully in a pair of old man's slippers, stopped, stared into the open doorway, went on, and came back to stand in the entrance. Her face, working with an effort at self-control, was suspicious.

Elizabeth noticed that one hand, drawn up in her shawl, was held close to her breast, and her shoulder was drawn up as if in pain.

"Could there be a doctor here?" said the woman.

She had spelled out the sign, and was looking about the room to see if anyone else beside Elizabeth was present. There was no one.

In sudden thought, she then screwed up her mouth and cocked her head sideways at Elizabeth. "It can't be yourself is the doctor!" she said. Her look was incredulous.

"It can be," said Elizabeth.

She spoke very quietly and without looking directly at the woman. She kept perfectly still, allowing the old woman to study her, as she sat at the desk seemingly occupied with some writing.

For a moment the room was absolutely quiet. Then Elizabeth looked up and spoke matter-of-factly. "Your arm hurts you, doesn't it?"

The old woman, still standing indecisively in the doorway, looked startled, and then her face puckered up.

"That it does," she said. She moved a step forward holding her hand to her shoulder. "I can neither sit, stand or lie," she said. "I don't know what to do with it all, I'm so miserable . . . !"

Elizabeth, still writing, looked up. "Does the pain shoot down into your arm, and into all of your fingers?"

The woman edged forward, sat down in the chair by the desk. "That it does! That it does . . ." And she began to talk eagerly of her symptoms.

When the old woman had been examined and treated, and was standing by the door again, she turned to Elizabeth. "Then you do know just like a proper doctor . . ." she said.

She was much impressed with the soothing plaster Elizabeth had applied to the sore shoulder, and with the advice that Elizabeth had given her.

"I *am* a proper doctor!" said Elizabeth.

"Then I will tell all my friends, and they will come to you!"

True to her word, the old woman returned a few days later leading a sick grandchild by the hand, and with her were several other patients, all women.

Elizabeth treated them all in turn, and by the end of the summer was quite busy, for not only did she take care of the patients who came, she also went out to the tenement homes of those who were too sick to be brought to the dispensary.

The neighborhood was one of the worst in the city. Sometimes at night, going and coming from the emergency calls that were now more frequent, she had unpleasant experiences. It was unheard of to see a woman about alone. Men, of course, followed her. But Elizabeth walked briskly, paid no attention, and manged somehow not to be afraid. To keep her composure was sometimes a problem. While waiting for a horsecar at midnight by the City Hall, a policeman, for the first time seeing a lone woman out at night, came up and tried to banter, reaching for her hand. But Elizabeth began to talk of the poor family she had visited, of the child desperately sick with scarlatina, with whom she had been sitting.

And looking full into the man's face she said, "My work of mercy would be impossible, if it were not for the chivalry of men like yourself, who respect it. I came to this corner," she went on, "because I knew fully that I could rely on your protection!"

And in passing that way again at night, she never again had trouble with this particular policeman.

Once, on lower Broadway, dark and deserted at night, she was walking very rapidly, because no omnibus was in sight, and cabs were a luxury she could not allow herself. Across the street a door opened and a group of late revellers coming into the street saw her.

"See that lone woman walking like mad!" they shouted.

But Elizabeth went on, did not for once look back, and their catcalls and whistlings after a while ceased.

Insolent anonymous letters came to her. She had no medical companionship, and except for the few Quaker friends she had made through Dr. Warrington's introductions, and through the efforts of her self-appointed patroness, Mrs. Hussey, she knew very few people, and had very few paying patients.

Before the summer was over, the few dollars provided for the support of the little dispensary had been spent, and so had all the savings which Elizabeth could spare for this purpose.

"This work," she wrote to her sister in Cleveland, "must be put on a sounder footing if it is to succeed."

She had tried to raise the money necessary to keep the dispensary open, but during the summer most of the women who might have contributed were out of the city. And she was forced, at last, just when the immigrant women had come to know and trust her, to close the little room on Tompkins Square for want of funds.

Some of her patients, on hearing that she would no longer be there, were desperate. And although she knew it would cause trouble at her lodgings at University Place, she gave them her address there, and poor as they were, lacking the money even for an omnibus ride, they would walk all the way from the river. Sometimes an immigrant woman would come with a child in her arms, quite exhausted, and Elizabeth would furnish the medicines and would pay out the pennies necessary to return them both home.

"There is the greatest need for this work," she wrote to Emily, who would soon complete her work at Western Reserve College and expected, as Elizabeth had done, to go to Europe for further study.

In the spring Emily arrived, to stay with Elizabeth for a few weeks, visit some of the New York hospitals and prepare for her journey.

"When I come back," said Emily, who was younger than Elizabeth, and who still looked up as always to her older sister, "I shall come directly to you and we shall work together."

Emily, slight like her sister, but far prettier with her soft, curling blond hair, and very fine features, had proven, nevertheless, a very serious medical student.

"Of all subjects," she said, talking with Elizabeth one evening in her room, "surgery interests me the most . . ."

Elizabeth sighed. "One of us, Emily," she said, "will have to be proficient in this field."

Sir James Simpson, the famous Scottish surgeon, who had

been lecturing at a New York hospital, and whom Elizabeth had approached, had promised to take the young woman medical student as an assistant, if she would come to Edinburgh.

"Those two years of training will be invaluable to you," advised Elizabeth.

And for a moment she envied her sister. She could not help thinking of the sad accident which had occurred at La Marternité, and of the illness that had followed afterwards, impairing her eyesight and destroying forever her hope of becoming a surgeon.

"My life will have to take other directions now," she said.

And later in the evening, when she was lying on the cot behind the screen, and her sister had gone to bed on the improvised sofa near the window, Elizabeth, awake in the dark, began to talk softly, as if she were speaking to herself.

"I am thirty-three years old," she said, "and I cannot go on living alone."

"Certainly you won't mean . . . !" Her sister was startled.

Elizabeth sat up. "No! No! Not that," she said quickly. "Of course I won't marry. It's quite impossible. Some day women will do the work that they want to and will have families, too. But for us, you and me, now in the beginning, one career is hard enough!" She sighed, talking over the screen in the dark and without being able to see her sister's face.

"What I mean to do is something else altogether. I'm going to adopt a child, Emily. . . ."

And she went on to tell her sister of a little girl, not quite eight years old, of unknown parentage, but no doubt of Irish birth, whom she had seen several times while visiting in the orphan asylum on Randall's Island.

"Her name is Kitty Barry," she said, "and she's very fond of me."

The next day Emily went with her to the orphan asylum, and when the matron admitted them, she seemed at once to know why Elizabeth had come. She went down the hall and returned immediately with a bright-faced little girl, with immense dark eyes, and black hair, who ran to Elizabeth impulsively.

"You have come again!" she cried.

Elizabeth knelt down and took the child's hand. "Would you like to come home with me? To take care of me, and let me take care of you?"

The child's face was solemn. "I will go," she said, "and I will take care of you all my life!"

Even the matron, whose face usually showed no expression, turned away.

For a week Emily and Elizabeth were busy sewing and stitching for the child, cooking meals on a spirit lamp behind the screen, and eating together on Elizabeth's desk, as she said, "like a proper family."

Elizabeth had unpacked an old box of books, the tales of Mrs. Mary Martha Butt Sherwood, which she had read as a child, and now she was teaching Kitty to read from them. It was delightful to see how the little girl responded to the first love she had evidently ever known, and how eagerly she waited for the sound of Elizabeth's footsteps, when she had gone out for a call.

"Are all women doctors?" she asked one evening, and made both women laugh.

"No," said Emily, "but I am going to be one."

"When I grow up," replied Kitty, looking up from the floor where she was playing with a doll that Elizabeth had given her, "I will not be a doctor. I will stay home and take care of you, and we will have many dogs to play with and a big, big house."

"Well, you see," said Elizabeth, "now I'm provided for."

On the evening before Emily's departure, the two sisters sat up very late.

"What is needed," said Elizabeth, who was talking as usual of the dispensary, which she had managed to reopen a few weeks before in another rented room, this time on Third Street, much nearer to the poor district in which she had become known. "What is needed," she said, "is really a woman's hospital, and a school, a school for nurses, and a school too where women physicians can be properly and thoroughly trained."

"Heavens," said Emily, "sometimes you frighten me!"

Elizabeth, impatient as usual when her sister showed the trait of caution which always had annoyed her, got up. Her face was almost angry. "What's the use of half-measures?" she cried. "When a thing has to be done, it has to be done!"

When Emily had been gone a few weeks, Elizabeth acquired an eager disciple. One evening, on returning from a late call, she found the gaslight burning in her room, and a visitor waiting.

It was a girl with a strong, sharp eager face and dressed very plainly. When she spoke, it was with such a strong German accent that at first Elizabeth could scarcely understand her.

Her name was Marie Zakrzewska, she said, and she had come all the way from Germany to America, because she wanted, as Elizabeth had done, to study medicine. For more than a year she had been living in an attic room in New York with her sister. Both girls supported themselves by doing sewing, factory piecework, any kind of work they could get. And every penny had been saved, so that Marie, who had dreamt about it from childhood, could start studying.

"Where shall I go? How shall I begin?" she said, explaining that the Society for the Friendless to whom she had gone for advice, had sent her to Elizabeth.

"This day will be God-sent for me!" she exclaimed when Elizabeth told her she must first learn to read and write English better and, engaged by the young girl's enthusiasm, offered not only to give her daily lessons in English, but in anatomy and in other medical subjects as well.

Every evening Marie came, and Elizabeth, returning from

her calls, would read a little while to Kitty, then sit down to work with her student.

Marie studied hard and advanced with amazing rapidity. By fall, Elizabeth was able to recommend her to the same school in Cleveland from which Emily had been graduated.

Marie also worked with Elizabeth in the dispensary. "Actual practice, the opportunity for observation is more valuable than all the lectures to which you can listen," young Dr. Blackwell told her pupil.

Marie left in the autumn for Cleveland, and a few weeks later, Elizabeth, writing to her sister Emily in England, could report of her young protégé, "She is studying with might and main, and will, I have no doubt, succeed; so we may reckon on a little group of three next year. . . ."

Already, she felt stronger in anticipation of the help that her sister and this eager young woman would give her. Marie would be a graduate doctor about the time that Emily, according to her letters, would be returning to America.

In the meantime, Elizabeth's practice was growing. She had opened her office in 1852, in the late summer. Now, writing to Emily just two years later, again in the summer, she could report, "With regard to my own clientele, I have advanced fifty dollars over last year, slow progress but still satisfactory."

Her circle of friends was larger, and there were people now who believed in her. But even her most ardent and enthusiastic friends could not agree with her when she began talking of a new project: a woman's hospital, to be run by a staff of women physicians, herself, Marie, and Emily.

There were so many insurmountable difficulties, it was pointed out to her. No one would rent a house for such a purpose. The female doctors would be looked upon with so much suspicion that even the police could not help them. And if a death should occur in the hospital, how could they issue a death certificate? Certainly it wouldn't be respected by the proper authorities. As for discipline, the discipline necessary with ignorant patients, how could women alone achieve it and control them?

Why there might even be mob action and violence! It would be risking their lives as well as their reputations! Elizabeth's friends tried to dissuade her.

She listened as usual, quite calmly, but was not swerved in the slightest degree from her purpose. If anything, criticism made her more adamant, more determined.

Malicious stories were circulated about her. She was a freak, touched with the mania of ambition, wanting to be a man instead of a woman! How else were such preposterous plans to be explained?

The stories were reported to Elizabeth. She listened to them, smiled, made no effort to refute them, seemed not to have been touched by the mischief behind them.

But in writing to her sister, she had to admit, "These malicious stories are painful to me, for I am a woman as well as physician, and both natures are wounded by these falsehoods."

Yet even as she wrote, the pain which the gossip caused seemed to soften.

Nothing which was said or done to her could really touch her. "Oh, I am glad," she went on in the letter to Emily, feeling this rising strength within herself, "that I, and not another, have to bear this pioneer work!"

After all there was a zest in breaking through, in making the way, in going in the direction exactly that she had planned.

"I understand now why this life has never been lived before," she concluded. "It is hard, with no support but a high purpose, to live against every species of social opposition. . . ."

But actually it was not hard, because a softer life would for her have been quite impossible!

CHAPTER NINE

AT LAST THE MEETING OF THE FAIR ASSOCIA-
tion was over, and the half dozen visiting ladies in their
swaying skirts and deep fashionable bonnets, their elaborate
curls and their big satin-flowered sewing bags, were gone.
And behind them, in the bare parlor of the still not completely furnished house on Fifteenth Street, where the meeting had been held, over a table littered with papers and
computations, sat three earnest young women.

Elizabeth, still scribbling, was the first to speak. "Ten
thousand dollars," she said, "is the sum. We can't open the
hospital with one penny less!"

"At the rate that those ladies are knitting . . ." burst out Marie, "I very much doubt that we'll ever raise ten thousand cents . . . let alone ten thousand dollars!"

She spoke almost wryly. Since being graduated from the medical school in Cleveland, Dr. Zakrzewska had come immediately to New York and had at once joined Elizabeth.

Emily, who was standing at Elizabeth's shoulder, looked down at the figure. "I wish," she said, that you could agree with me. I do believe we could get started in a much smaller way."

On her return from Europe, where she had completed her training under the great surgeon, Dr. Simpson, Emily had come to New York too, and straight to her sister, of course, whom she found not at the old address, in rented lodgings, but in a house of her own on Fifteenth Street.

"Nowhere else," explained Elizabeth "and under no other conditions, could I get the privilege of hanging out a sign."

There were three signs on the door now: Elizabeth's, Marie's, and Emily's. "Now we are our own landlords!"

But she did not tell either Emily or her friend, Marie, of the struggles she had been through. How it had been necessary to borrow money for the first payment on the house. How she had been obliged to let all the rooms to a family that kept lodgers, sleeping in the attic herself, borrowing the use of the parlor and a screen so that she could receive her few patients, with some show of privacy.

All that was over now. She could take care of the house, and had written to her sister Marion and to her mother, asking that they come to live with her. The old home in Cincinnati was broken up. Henry was married at last to the indomitable Lucy Stone, with whom, in the old-fashioned parlor of her father's house, he had signed a pact of equality, allowing his wife to retain her maiden name. Together they moved to New Jersey where he was engaged in the book business, participating also in the growing movement for women's rights for which his wife fought so ardently.

Marion, who had visited with them, was ill again, and wanted to be near Elizabeth. "I'm never afraid when I'm near you," she said to her sister.

And Kitty, the little Irish girl whom Elizabeth had adopted, and who was so devoted to her, was leaving the boarding school to which she had been sent and was coming home to live.

With all these responsibilities, with the payments that had to be met on the house, and the bills which had to be worried about, Elizabeth still had energy for new and ambitious plans.

In 1854, soon after the Tompkins Square dispensary had closed for lack of funds, Elizabeth asked the legislature and secured from the state of New York a charter for a woman's hospital. The new institution, to be known as the New York Infirmary for Women and Children, would be both a dispensary and a hospital with public wards. To maintain it, for the opening period of three years, the sum of ten thousand dollars was necessary according to Elizabeth's figures.

"I do think," repeated Emily, "that we ought to be satisfied to start with less—much less!"

"And close again as I did in the little dispensary, for want of funds to go on? Oh no!" cried Elizabeth. "This time we'll raise the money, all of it that's needed, and then we'll begin!"

She had organized a Fair Association, a group of women who met weekly to sew and knit on gift articles later to be sold at a fair or bazaar. This was an accepted way of raising money and the abolitionist societies were continually holding events of this kind.

"Shall we have two ladies or two-and-a-half at our sewing circle today?" mocked Marie.

Elizabeth looked at her sharply. "It's our own fault," she said. "We've given them nothing tangible to work for!"

"What else can we do?" said Emily. "We have no money."

"We can get a building, and then we can work to pay for it!" was Elizabeth's astounding reply.

Two days later she announced that she had found a house, a fine old-fashioned residence on Bleecker Street, "and which will be," she declared, "exactly suitable for our purpose!"

The yearly rental was one thousand three hundred dollars, with a lease required for no less than three years!

"Four thousand dollars!" gasped Emily. "It's madness. We'll never raise such a sum!"

And even Marie was frightened.

"Small sum or big sum, the difficulties are the same," replied Elizabeth, and to the board of trustees and the Fair Association called together at a joint meeting, she announced that she proposed taking the house.

"We will open the New York Infirmary for Women and Children there one year from today, on the date of May 1, 1857!"

Her enthusiasm convinced the members, who began at once discussing who should be the speakers at the opening, and what kind of ceremony should be performed. Everyone was in favor of Dr. Henry Ward Beecher as the speaker.

"Dr. Beecher it will be!" said Elizabeth, and sent off the letter inviting him to be present.

The vitriolic preacher, who had auctioned off a slave girl from his pulpit, raising two thousand dollars in the space of ten minutes, would not be amazed to be solicited as master of ceremonies for an institution which did not yet exist, for which not a single penny had been collected.

"Of course I will come," he replied. What other answer could be expected from Harriet Beecher Stowe's brother?

Even Emily became enthusiastic. Marie was sent off to Boston with a letter to Dr. Harriet Kezia Hunt, the self-trained woman physician, and the pledge to raise two thousand dollars there for the hospital. Elizabeth promised to match, perhaps to exceed, this amount in New York contributions.

She had always been a good speaker. Emily and a committee of ladies were kept busy arranging groups before whom she could appear. She spoke in drawing rooms, at Sunday schools, before abolitionist and other liberal societies.

Not all groups were friendly. Many people questioned the need for a new charity, when the Union trembled on the brink of disaster, the Southern states threatened to secede, and the evils of slavery grew each day more threatening.

"There is more misery in the Eleventh Ward which we are going to serve," Elizabeth would reply, "than on any Southern plantation!"

"War or no war, slavery or not, we are responsible also for the suffering in our midst—and which threatens us!" She spoke of "the fever nests" that existed in rotting tenements. "There's no fence to be built round infection," she cried, and told of the diseases bred in this poorest of all immigrant districts, "and carried with each wind that blows to your wives and your children!"

She could be dramatic, matter-of-fact, deeply appealing, as the occasion required. Her voice, for anyone so slight, was amazingly deep and full, and she could handle an audience without difficulty.

She was never self-conscious, had no sense of personal appearance, and went about without the slightest vanity, in an old bonnet and a gown which had no pretensions of style.

"How can you appear before people in such a costume?" her mother cried one day as she was leaving. "Your gown is rusty, and your bonnet . . ." she threw up her hands.

Elizabeth turned to her calmly. "Then by all means I shall have to put on my most assuming manner!" she said.

It was true that she had no time now to go looking through the shining white emporiums of Twenty-third Street for a wardrobe. She was everywhere at once, everywhere

successful; speaking, soliciting pledges, interviewing carpenters, furniture makers, painters. Everything depended on her, nothing could be decided without her. When the Fair Committee failed to secure a hall for their event, because it seemed no one wanted to rent to women, she flew at once into action.

"Mr. Haydock," she said, calling on this gentleman in his office at 46 Broadway, near the Bowery, "you will absolutely have to find us a loft, any kind of loft. There's no church that will rent to us and no landlord that will have us."

She knew that he had control of some properties. "But all that I have is this," he told her, as she climbed three dusty flights of stairs with him, to a vast, gloomy attic. "It can hardly be suitable."

The loft was unfinished, with rough walls, a floor full of knotholes, no lighting fixtures. Still it was located in the business district.

"We'll take it," said Elizabeth.

And in three weeks' time, under her direction, the room was transformed. There were rugs on the floor, borrowed from the ladies, hangings and decorations of ivy and evergreen on the walls, and even a beautiful parlor chandelier, inveigled from a not-so-willing member of the committee, had been connected to a gas jet, and illumined beautifully the long tables, the hundreds of gift items laid out for display; antimacassars drawn through with ribbons, rainbow shawls, painted dishes, figurines of gilt, fancy saucers, collars of lace and crochet—a true gift emporium and opening just at the right time, three weeks before Christmas!

The sale opened, lasted for three days, and brought in the sum of six hundred dollars. The drive for contributions continued, and in the house on Bleecker Street, among pots of paint and piles of fresh shavings, Elizabeth was busy accomplishing miracles with a crew of recalcitrant workmen.

At last the alterations were made. The front and back parlors were thrown together to make wards. In the little hall bedroom, the small window was taken out, was replaced with a large, high, many-paned glass to light what was to be the operating theatre—a tiny room, but replete with all of Emily's instruments.

The bedsteads were installed, the mattresses were put into sacking. The linens were hemmed, and the curtains stiff with starch were tied back from the window sills on which plants had been placed—for it was Elizabeth's theory that above all, the wards must be sunny, homelike and cheerful.

"If people aren't happy, they can't get well," she said, remembering the bleak walls of Blockley.

The medical supplies were brought in, Elizabeth contributed her precious hoard, so did Emily; and the textbooks of the three women were disposed on a white shelf with a curtain below it—the beginnings of the hospital library!

On an afternoon in May, as Elizabeth had predicted, in the old-fashioned drawing room, now turned into a snowy ward, the opening ceremonies were held. A handful of earnest men and women were present, including Dr. Beecher, who made the opening remarks; Dr. Elder of Philadelphia; Mr. Horace Greeley of the *Tribune;* Miss Mary Booth whose unsigned articles in the *New York Times* had been so helpful; Mr. Collins, Mr. Haydock, Cornelia Hussey, and a few of the other most zealous workers.

Elizabeth conducted them on a tour through the building. Below, on the first floor, set off from the large room which was to serve as the dispensary, were the three little offices of the physicians. Above were two spacious wards, each holding eight beds, with room for more if the need should arise. On the top floor, which was divided into tiny cubicles, were quarters for nurses and internes.

"These most certainly will be needed some day," said Elizabeth, and not stopping for the looks of surprise which she encountered, she went on to say that it was her intention that both a school of nursing and a school to train women as physicians should grow naturally out of the work of the hospital.

Marie had been appointed resident physician. Emily, who had the title of surgeon, had already shown her competence in this work. In addition, she had a real talent for management. After her first opposition to Elizabeth's plans which were always more bold than her cautious nature would allow, she would settle down to carrying out every smallest detail with the greatest possible care.

It had been a home-saying when they were children that "Elizabeth begins, Emily continues!" And it was true that they supplemented each other remarkably, even though sometimes there were conflicts. On these occasions it was usually Elizabeth's stronger will that prevailed, although sometimes when events were against her, she did yield to Emily.

There was the matter of the woman's medical college, for example, for which Elizabeth began to plan even before the hospital was opened. "We shall need physicians," she said, "women who are properly trained and can do the work that is needed!"

She did not think much of the rather inadequate courses given at the Philadelphia Medical College for Women, and at a new school which had sprung up in Boston.

"What is wanted," she declared, "is a thorough course, full and complete, lasting at least four years!"

Her sister was amazed. Most medical schools, having increased their terms to three years, thought they were giving the very maximum in the way of training.

"You don't mean to exceed that?"

"Why not?" said Elizabeth. "We shall set them an example," and she spoke as though the school were an immediate possibility, about to be established tomorrow.

"We shall create a chair of hygiene," she said. "We shall for the first time in the history of medicine teach what I believe is the most important subject of all—the prevention of disease!"

This was an idea about which she talked constantly. It interested her more than any other aspect of medicine. To teach the immigrant families cleanliness, to have doctors and trained nurses who would go into their homes, showing them how to prepare food, how to prevent infection, how to nurse, how to live. . . . She had seen so much misery as she climbed the dirty stairs of crowded tenements, sitting up nights with sick patients in hot, airless attics or in miserable cellars where no human being could possibly recover.

Misery, ignorance, filth, these were diseases as dreadful as any she had treated. And the only medicine was to educate, educate ceaselessly and according to a definite plan. She had seen the blankets of a child, sick with scarlet fever, shaken into an air shaft opening on rooms below where other children slept. She knew of households where the one dark, crowded kitchen was workroom, bedroom and living quarters for a family who worked from morning till night, making cigars, doing piecework, and their total earnings could not supply better food for the children than bread and coffee!

Every year the immigrant ships came, every year brought new cartloads of misery. Every year cholera raged in New York, starting always in the crowded tenement districts near the river, and typhus, the dreadful ship fever, which she had seen take such a toll in her student days at Blockley.

Elizabeth learned the tongues of the immigrant women, German, Bohemian, Italian, Slavic, and spoke to them half in signs, half in gestures. Bewildered, they came running to the "big house" on Bleecker Street, stood for hours with their sick children in their arms, waiting for their turn at the dispensary. And Elizabeth, climbing the stairs to their shabby rooms, taught them the newer and cleaner ways of living, how to air their bedclothes on a sunny fire escape, how to cook more healthful foods, how to give the few simple medicines she prescribed, and above all she taught them to come early when they were sick.

"Do not wait," she would warn, "until it is too late for us to help you!"

By the end of the year, three hundred patients had been treated, and the State Legislature, taking cognizance, at last, of the woman's institution, voted a fund of $750.00 to help in its support. Upon Elizabeth's insistence to the City Council, this body, too, voted an allotment for the support of charity patients treated at the hospital.

The three women worked days, nights, on Sundays, on holidays. They were fund-raisers, doctors, housekeepers and also nurses in turn. Finally it was possible to hire a girl, Miss Louise Ryckman, who would do only the nursing. Her wages were eight dollars a week. And Elizabeth, training the plump, blond German girl in some simple procedures of the sickroom, remembered the talks she had had at Embley Park with her friend, Florence Nightingale.

"The time has come to start a school where nurses can be trained scientifically," she now declared.

She planned a three-month course, advertised in the papers for volunteers, and with the four girls who enlisted, and who came to live in the little cubicles in the attic, she started the first nursing school in America. Years were to pass before Bellevue, New York's largest hospital, was to copy her plan, importing one of Miss Nightingale's "nursing sisters" to inaugurate the work there.

The girls who were trained at the Infirmary were carefully chosen. "We must look for character and heart first," said Elizabeth.

When a young woman in a bold bloomer costume applied, Elizabeth took one look at her short, clipped hair, at her cherry-red pantaloons and exotic jacket, and rejected her.

She had no use for the "women's rights" agitators of this type, flamboyant, calling attention to themselves, harming the cause. There was her sister-in-law, Lucy Stone, working in the forefront of this movement with her husband, Henry; and yet, how quiet, how unassuming and how deeply gentle she was in spite of all her accomplishments.

And Elizabeth's brother, Samuel, had also married a feminist, Antoinette Browne, a classmate of Lucy's, the first woman to be graduated from the theological course at Oberlin, and the first woman to be ordained a minister. Yet even Mrs. Blackwell said that no one could have equalled this kind woman's tact and manners.

The real workers for the cause of women were women first: tiny Lucretia Mott, Lucy who was so human that all causes interested her, Antoinette with her deep devotion to her husband and children.

"When women have cured prejudice, they will have cured the worst of all diseases!" Dr. Beecher had said in his opening remarks at the Infirmary.

There were many prejudices still. The way for the three women at the Infirmary was still hard, still paved with troubles.

On the occasion of the first operation to be performed at the hospital, Emily who was about to operate, and the sick woman who was growing more nervous every minute, were kept waiting a whole hour while a surgeon of the city, who had promised to come and be present as a consultant, hesitatingly conferred with a medical colleague "on the propriety of attending an operation performed by a woman!"

The operation was performed, the patient recovered, but the relatives of the sick woman could not be persuaded that the results were as good as they might have been. After all, how could a woman be a physician!

This suspicion of their competence, of their ability, only because they were women, never ceased to trouble the doctors of the Infirmary. The could try their best. But people still would ask—would it not have been better if the doctor had been a man? And if a patient was lost, as had to happen inevitably when so many difficult cases were handled, then the feeling always rose up that if a man doctor had been consulted, perhaps the patient after all would have been saved. And on two occasions, there were really very ugly scenes, with both the hospital and the lives of the women physicians being put in danger.

A woman had died of inflammation of the appendix, a condition for which there was no known cure and no known method of treatment. Elizabeth had warned the relatives of the slight hope for recovery. All through the night, they had lined the walls of the sickroom, coming and going like ghosts. Towards morning, for the night had been very hot, they went down on the lawn to wait. A half hour later, Elizabeth, opening the front door, made a motion.

A woman whom Elizabeth recognized as a sister of the patient sprang up from the grass. "You killed her!" she cried.

The others at once began to scream and lament, accusing Elizabeth, accusing the hospital, accusing women doctors in general.

Neighbors stuck their heads out of the windows, passersby came running, and in no time at all such a crowd had gathered that Elizabeth, who tried to speak, could not make herself heard at all. There was nothing to do but go inside, bolt the door against the rioters who were now threatening all sorts of things—that they would break down the doors and ransack the building.

"They're only women—what right do they have to set themselves up as physicians!"

The rioting continued for more than an hour, stones were thrown, insults were shouted, and inside the patients were hysterical.

Finally a young physician, Dr. Richard Sharpe Kissam,

who served as consultant for the hospital, came running, managed somehow to climb through the crowd, and making his way to the husband of the dead woman, offered at once to perform an autopsy to prove that all proper care had been taken.

"That's reasonable!" shouted someone. "But if all is not well then most certainly we'll come back!"

Finally the crowd dispersed, the relatives were taken inside, the examination was made, and it was shown to everyone's complete satisfaction that the cause of death had been inevitable. Both the hospital and the women physicians were completely cleared.

Taking the hand of the grief-stricken husband, Elizabeth spoke gently. "You could not help yourself," she said, "we women doctors have, after all, come before our time!"

Marie was incensed at the indignity the hospital had suffered. But Elizabeth was obsessed by another feeling altogether. She thought of the dead woman. When would medicine cease to be helpless in such cases? Later, when she lost a little boy patient, she was equally depressed.

"How little we know! How little we are able to do!" she cried to Emily.

When another grave case was brought to the hospital, followed by another death, an even worse commotion was caused by the relatives who were street workers and day laborers. Assembled on the lawn with their pickaxes and their shovels, they shouted imprecations and insults, barricading the building on all sides.

Marie, leaning out to call for help, was greeted with a cloud of stones. Emily ran from window to window drawing the shutters. Elizabeth had her hands full to keep the hysterical patients from jumping out of their beds.

"We'll be destroyed altogether!" cried Marie. She was overwrought from working fifteen hours a day, and was suffering with nervous headaches.

"Be quiet," said Elizabeth. "We'll endure it and after a time they'll stop!"

In the wards her calmness had the effect of making the patients quiet at once.

Now the battering on the door suddenly ceased, and so did the noise outside. Elizabeth ran up to the second floor, opened a window cautiously, looked out. Someone was speaking. A big burly man, whom Elizabeth recognized as one of her former patients, had mounted the steps, was barring the way to the doorway.

She remembered his case well. He had been ill with an attack of pneumonia. Now he was telling the crowd how she had saved him. He was an Irishman, emotional, and could speak well.

"Only the Lord has the power of life and death," he pleaded.

Then he went on to speak of the good that had been done for his friends and for his neighbors by these women doctors. Now another man stepped out from the crowd. His family, too, had been helped. Why, in the middle of the night the woman doctor had come when his baby was sick with the croup, and they had no money for medicines and did not know where they could get help!

In the midst of the second man's speech, a policeman came running from Bleecker Street, another one from Broadway. Both men knew Elizabeth, both had seen her at night, in lonely neighborhoods, going and coming in districts which even a man would not have entered alone.

They appealed to the mob in turn, finally prevailing upon the relatives to take the proper course of action—calling for the coroner, and asking for an inquest, if they had the slightest suspicion of the care that had been taken.

Again an inquest was held and again the hospital was cleared of all responsibility, "all care and precautions that are possible having been taken in the case!" Dr. Gallagher, a city official, gave the report, shook hands afterwards with Elizabeth. "You have," he said, "a much harder time than some!"

Elizabeth laughed. "We should be used to it by now," she said. "It's only when educated people are against us that I'm a little bit startled!"

The week before she had gone with Marie to call upon Fanny Kemble, the famous English actress who had come to New York to give a series of Shakespearean readings. Her purpose was to ask the great tragedienne, whom she had met once at the home of Lady Byron, if she would not give a performance for the benefit of the Infirmary's charity fund.

The actress listened to her courteously enough, until it became clear to her that the institution was run by women. At this information, when it was perfectly clear to her that the physicians were women, she sprang to her full height, turned her flashing eyes on Elizabeth, and with the deepest most tragic tones of her magnificent voice exclaimed: "Trust a *woman*—as a doctor!—Never!"

It was after this incident that Emily, in discussing with Elizabeth the project of a medical school, ventured the opinion that it would be better to wait until people were less prejudiced. After all, there was public opinion to consider. . . .

"Public opinion," said Elizabeth crisply, "should be *made*, not followed!"

Afterwards both sisters, laughing, agreed that it was an aphorism good enough to present to an audience.

"The trouble, Mother," Emily complained afterwards, "is that Elizabeth just can't stop, can't ever leave well enough alone."

Kitty, almost thirteen now, tall and grave, with black hair arranged in side curls, fixed her blue, vivid eyes on Elizabeth, whose part she always took. "Why should it be impossible?" she said.

"Don't you see, Emily," went on Elizabeth, glancing at the young girl, "that it's inevitable? There's no school in the country that will properly train women. And if we, as pioneers, allow poor physicians to be turned out, then the whole sex will be discredited!"

And she would have gone on with her plans except for new events which offered now even a greater distraction than before.

Up the Bowery one day had moved a strange apparition, a figure on stilts, twenty feet high, dressed in spectral clothes and trailing a banner which read, "Let no man put asunder the Union that God hath formed!" It was called the "phantom of disunion," and was meant to warn of inevitable events, events about which everyone talked, everyone feared, and about which no one, for all the bitterness that was rampant, could do anything.

The war would come. How could it be avoided? Lincoln would be elected. The Southern states would secede, and then, would come the struggle.

"The worst war the country has ever seen, the bloodiest and the most terrible!"

"This is no time, no time at all for waging private campaigns," warned Emily.

Dr. Zakrzewska had retired from the Infirmary, going to Boston to take a post as a lecturer at the Female College of Medicine. A new resident physician, a young woman, Dr. Annette Buckel, had been appointed to her place, and another young woman, Dr. Mary E. Breed, had, with Elizabeth's training, become an assistant.

The work was growing, was gradually being accepted. Where 300 patients had been treated at the Infirmary during the first year, ten times that number came and were cared for the following year. The famous promoter of the telegraph cable, Mr. Cyrus Field, said he felt himself honored to be named as a trustee of the woman's institution, and from abroad had come eminent physicians to visit the Infirmary, study the case records and note the methods of work.

"A most interesting departure," they called Elizabeth's latest innovation, an "out-patient service," planned to carry on the care of patients in their homes after they had left the hospital. It was an ambitious plan, to go into people's homes, to make their lives over, to teach them how to keep well, to erase the causes of disease—before ever they occurred!

"Most drastic! Most revolutionary!" A few understood, even though some thought Elizabeth's work visionary. But the news of what she had done had spread, was hailed in England with far more enthusiasm than at home. From her English friends, from the Bracebridges, from Lady Byron, from the noted worker for charity, Countess de Noalles, came letters asking that she take a year of leave and come to England for the purpose of aiding in the campaign to start a woman's hospital there—a hospital modeled after the Infirmary.

At first she was unwilling to go. But Emily was so reliable, so completely competent, now that there were no innovations at the Infirmary. And Kitty could be left in Mrs. Blackwell's care. The little girl was devoted to Elizabeth, and talked continually of the time when she would be grown up and could help "Dr. Elizabeth" who worked so hard, thought so little of herself.

It was hard to leave the child, for the little girl had grown into Elizabeth's life. With her calm, sweet temperament and soothing manner, so grave, so mature already, she supplemented the older woman in amazing ways. "She fits Elizabeth's angles like an eiderdown quilt." This was a family saying, and it expressed the relationship exactly.

She said good-bye to the child at the dock, had some anxious nights in crossing, and arrived in London in the summer of 1858, to spend a busy year. She did not return to

America until the war at home so long expected was really imminent. And her letters throughout the whole time were enthusiastic.

"There is an immense charm in this fresh field," she wrote. "I like working and living in England, and there is no limit to what we might accomplish here!"

She gave a series of lectures in Manchester, in Liverpool, in Birmingham, and at the Marylebone Literary Institute in London. Everywhere she was received enthusiastically, everywhere given the greatest honors. Her name was enrolled on the medical register of Great Britain—the name of the first woman in history to go down on this record. She was told by men and women of social distinction that if she should undertake to practice in London, the most notable people would come to her.

To Emily she wrote with enthusiasm. "On all hands we make converts, and those who are indoctrinated make converts. The whole way in which the cause is regarded . . . is most respectful. I believe we could get into general practice."

Elizabeth went to Malvern, for a visit with her old friend Florence Nightingale. She found her shockingly changed, frail, burnt out by the indescribable labors of the Crimea which had made her famous, her cause accepted overnight.

Florence Nightingale had set up miles of beds for the wounded, had accomplished such miracles with her handful of women, that no one thought now to question the competence of women as nurses. Her report on army conditions had been published by the British government. She had been honored by the Queen. Now she was immersed in plans for establishing a series of schools to train women scientifically for the care of the sick.

Again, as she had done in the beginning, she appealed to Elizabeth to work with her. In the old Embley Park days, discontented with the social life upon which her parents insisted, Florence had exclaimed one day to Elizabeth, "If you were to work with me, I would be perfectly happy."

The feeling of friendship, of complete understanding between these two women, had not ceased. Nevertheless collaboration was impossible.

"Unfortunately," wrote Elizabeth to her sister, "she does not think private practice possible in connection with her plan!"

The plans for the English hospital meanwhile went forward. A brilliant committee met: Lady Byron, the Honorable Russell Gurney, Mr. William Shaen, Dr. Charles Mayo. A circular was drawn up, petitions were sent out, and an intensive campaign, centered around Elizabeth's appearance on the lecture platform, was planned.

She spoke two and three nights a week, met with groups of volunteers, attended benefits, charities, social events. "The more I see of work in England," she wrote, "the more I like it. From the Queen downwards there are signs of favor."

And yet, in spite of this warm reception, the work went slowly, contributions were small, the results of the drives were meager. What it had taken seven years to accomplish in America, could not be accomplished in as many months in London.

To Emily in a final letter written before her departure Elizabeth had to make the admission. "Slow, uphill work, a repetition to a great extent of our last seven years' work at home is necessary here. It would need us both to do it well; and so greatly does England want just our experience, that if it were possible, I should counsel the transference of our work to this side of the water.

"But this we cannot do . . . so I shall endeavor to prepare others for the English work by receiving and educating students in America!"

Again her thoughts were reverting to plans for the school.

But returning in August, she found the Infirmary crowding out of its old quarters. Immediately she was busy raising funds, finding a location, planning for new furnishings and supplies. The old house had to be sold, and a new and more spacious building had to be found.

At the new location, Number 126 Second Avenue, closer to the river, and closer to the poor neighborhoods which the Infirmary served, Elizabeth was able to allot space for a school. A number of young women had come to her in London, promising that the moment the new school was opened, they would cross the Atlantic to enroll immediately.

"It is most imperative," she said to Emily, "that we should begin!"

But the firing on Fort Sumter put a hush over the city. All plans ceased. Then London called for men. Old dissensions broke out. There were men and women in New York who were still in favor of the South, still against the Negroes and the abolitionists. The draft law was passed. Mobs rioted in the streets, and in some quarters of the city colored people were injured and their homes ransacked.

At the Infirmary there was a colored woman in one of the wards. The other patients became so excited that they refused to stay in the same room with her. Elizabeth went up at once, spoke quietly but with the same firmness that had made it possible for her at seventeen to quell a whole classroom with a look.

"If there is anyone here who does not wish to remain, we will make arrangements . . . But, if it is your desire to stay, please remember that we have no room for intolerance here!"

Upon the request of some of the lady friends of the Infirmary, she called a meeting of volunteers for war work in her office. A notice got somehow into the *New York Times* and so many women came that they could not be accommodated. Accordingly a second and larger meeting was called for the next day at the Cooper Institute.

It was at this meeting that two important wartime organizations were formed: the National Sanitary Aid Association and the Ladies Sanitary Commission; one to look after the comforts of the soldiers, the other to furnish and train nurses for the war.

The volunteers for nursing work came flocking. Elizabeth passed on the applicants at the Infirmary, then they were sent on to Bellevue Hospital for the course of training which took three months. Women who were younger than thirty were not accepted as volunteers.

But one day, Kitty, who was assisting Elizabeth with the rush of enrollments, made a laughing comment. "I have never seen so many young women who were thirty, at least that's what they say they are, and yet look so obviously eighteen!"

And it was true that many young women were applying, making false declarations of their age. One of these volunteers, a delicate-looking girl, whom Elizabeth would have rejected except for the girl's pleading, was to prove herself a heroine. At Gettysburg, in men's boots, wading alone for two days and two nights through the mud and the blood of the battlefield, she was to rescue the still living men from among the terrible piles of the dead.

Refugees from the war found their way to New York and to the Infirmary. All were treated with the same kindness and concern, the same impartiality.

"Suffering does not take sides," said Elizabeth.

Widows of Confederate soldiers and of the men of the North were put to bed side by side in the wards which were now always crowded. Sometimes beds had to be set in the aisles. And those, who were not fully recovered yet, had to make way for the still more desperately ill. From the Boston Women's College and from the Philadelphia school, young women internes came to serve at the Infirmary. But Elizabeth was never contented with their training.

"We have not visualized yet," she said, "the true medical school!"

And she talked of curriculums and courses.

All the hectic work of the war years which made Emily sharper, and had also impaired Elizabeth's health at last, had not after all altered the plan to which she had held so steadily.

The battles of Antietam, Vicksburg, and Richmond echoed through the country, and almost simultaneously with the coming of peace came Elizabeth's last and final accomplishment for the Infirmary. On April 13, 1864, the New York State Legislature had voted an enabling act for a woman's medical college. And two years later, with an enrollment of fifteen students, the new school opened!

The course was to be one of four years' extent as Elizabeth had planned. There was no droning of lectures. All recitation, all instruction was to be personal. And for the first time in the history of American medicine, the subject of disease prevention was taught. Elizabeth occupied the chair of hygiene.

The school grew rapidly and so did the recognition of women in the profession of medicine. Celebrating the twentieth anniversary of her own graduation, Elizabeth could declare that "throughout the Northern States the free and equal entrance of women into the profession of medicine has been secured. In Boston, New York, and Philadelphia special medical schools for women were sanctioned by the Legislatures, and in some long-established colleges women are received as students in the ordinary classes!

"The pioneer work in America is ended," she said, and thinking over this sentence later, when she was alone in her room, Elizabeth understood now the growing restlessness which had puzzled her.

To simply run a smoothly-operating institution, a successful college, a recognized hospital, with trustees and public cooperating, was to her nature, which still demanded vigorous action, exceedingly dull. Emily, who was such a fine executive when the ground once was broken and the work laid out, could be happy and useful as head of the hospital and director of the fast-growing college. There would be no new problems, no new opposition in an organization well planned, stoutly started. And Elizabeth, like those pioneers of the West who feel impelled to move on, as soon as the land behind them is broken, began to understand why when she was successful and happy at last, she was at the same time so miserable.

"It's my nature," she said, "to start anew," and to Emily she confided that she was going to England. "What is done here is done. I can leave it."

But her presence in England, at a time when the pioneer work of women physicians was just beginning there, would, she felt, be of immeasurable assistance.

Emily, aghast at first, refused to countenance Elizabeth's plans. Yet gradually the arrangements were made, the ties were loosened, and at last the day of departure was set. Emily was to take over Elizabeth's duties as manager of the hospital and as director of the school. Elizabeth, as she announced to an amazed board of trustees, was retiring.

At the dock, among the trunks, she turned to her sister. "I couldn't do this, I couldn't go on, if I didn't have you to leave behind. . . ."

"The reliable and the prosaic half," said Emily, but her lips trembled.

They shook hands without speaking, two grave middle-aged women. And then Elizabeth leaned over, put her hands on her sister's shoulders, and kissed her.

From the rail of the ship she looked down. "Good-bye! Good-bye!" Kitty, standing beside her, was waving, weeping too a little in an excited sort of way. The young girl had wanted to go, but at the last moment was regretful.

The dock moved away. The rooftops grew distant, the outlines of the bay and of the islands seemed to melt. The sky was blue and gulls dipped after the ship.

Elizabeth, standing still at the rail, had a remembrance. She was a little girl again, holding her father's hand. They were standing at the rail of a ship, and the shoreline of Bristol, too, was melting into the blue sky where the wheeling gulls grew every moment fainter and fainter.

She turned abruptly, spoke brusquely to Kitty, and went down to her stateroom.

CHAPTER TEN

I COULD UNDERSTAND OPPOSITION MUCH BET-
ter," said Elizabeth as she got out of the carriage.

She was returning with Kitty from an evening party at
the home of Madame Bodichon, a famous London hostess,
and together they were discussing the notable people that
had been there, and the reception they had given Elizabeth.

George Eliot, the authoress, better known to her friends
as "Mrs. Lewes," had been present; Herbert Spencer, the
sociologist; Dante Gabriel Rossetti, the Cheyne Walk poet.

Mrs. Lewes had talked with Elizabeth for over an hour
about women and their work in medicine. Slight, eccentric,
dressed in old-fashioned hoops, her face framed by glossy
curls, she had fixed vivid eyes on Elizabeth and had ques-

tioned her intently. What did Dr. Blackwell think of the new scientific discoveries? What about Louis Pasteur and his theory of "sub-visible" beings? Could it be possible that diseases were actually caused by germs? Could women be surgeons? Could they be scientists? What could they contribute as physicians?

And Elizabeth, stimulated by the other's interest and keen knowledge, was kept busy answering.

Around them a circle had gathered. Mr. Spencer, the sociologist, interrupting after a time, expressed the view that the equality of the sexes would have to be taken for granted.

To this remark, Mr. Rossetti, with his mellow, mellifluous voice, took exception. "I wonder," he said, "if the practice of so gruesome a work as medicine might not rob women of their charm?"

Immediately there were defenders for Elizabeth. Was the American lady not charming, even though she was a physician?

Charles Kingsley, the writer, was presented; a warm, genial person with an amazing humility, he took Elizabeth's hand enthusiastically, "Madam," he said, "you are one of my heroes!" And Elizabeth did not know what to answer.

Talking over all this enthusiasm with Kitty, when they were home again at Number 6, Burwood Place where she had taken consultation rooms, Elizabeth made a practical comment.

"It's all very gratifying, this good feeling," she said, drawing off her gloves and going at once to her study table, "but it's a great pity that it can't somehow be put to practical use!"

She was thinking of the hospital for women that was needed so badly in London . . . the college to teach medicine . . . the society she hoped to found for the purpose of keeping people well.

But for the first time in her life, with all the avenues, all

the opportunities open to her, she had to hold back. Soon
after coming to London she had been ill, very ill, an illness
brought on she knew by years of overwork, years of campaigning. And on recovering, she had promised herself,
promised Kitty, "no fund-raising, no outside work!"

Kitty, now twenty-three, acted as her secretary, took from
her whatever burdens she could, refused all night calls,
which were designated to a younger physician, and declined
the many invitations that asked Elizabeth to speak.

In the winter of 1870, Elizabeth, however, becoming very
impatient with the routine of calls, consultations, and parties, took on a piece of the serious work that she loved. She
agreed to give a series of lectures at the "Working Women's
College."

She was tired of fashionable people, she declared. "Their
lives," she said, "are not real and neither are their illnesses!"

Here would be serious listeners, who needed her advice.
She prepared a series of talks on the subject of *How to Keep
a Household in Health*. And to the working women and
housewives who came to listen, she gave blunt, frank, simple
advice.

She was amazed when her speech was misquoted, and
being reprinted in the papers, brought down a flood of insolent, insulting letters.

In no time at all, everyone in London had heard about
the incident, and everyone took sides. Elizabeth might not
have taken the matter seriously, if it had not been for the
concern of her friends.

Mr. Kingsley, the novelist, came to call. "I hope," he said,
"that you did not answer those letters!"

Elizabeth assured him that she hadn't.

"Thank God for that!" he exclaimed, and went on to tell
her how some of the cheap English papers created a scandal in this way. "They will go to any length in order to sell
more papers," he said. "Silence and your own established

character," he warned her, "are your only weapons." And he suggested that she should curtail, for the time being, any further public appearances.

But Elizabeth, who was quite used to attacks, made arrangements to give another series of lectures, this time at St. George's Hall. Her subject was *The Religion of Health*, and the advice that she gave aroused members of the medical profession and the press, much as her earlier talks had aroused the general public.

She attacked drugs and doctors, saying newfangled remedies would never take the place of sound prevention. To teach people how to keep well—that, she insisted, was the doctor's greater responsibility. And she predicted that the time would come when physicians would be teachers, and diseases would be cured—before they ever occurred!

She talked about sunshine, good food, freedom from worry. And to audiences used to the new and dramatic cures, her advice sounded almost too simple. Anesthetics had made operations painless. Sir Joseph Lister's great discoveries robbed the surgeon's knife of its dangers. Pasteur's vaccines had conquered terrifying infections. Elizabeth's idea of preventing sickness seemed, as one critic had said, "vague and weak by comparison!"

"It may be," she answered in reply, "that I am writing for the year 1970," and she made arrangements to have the talks on health put out in the form of a book.

The new creed of prevention must be understood, and must be accepted! In her drawing room, she called together, one evening, a group of men and women, chosen friends, trusted believers in her ideas. And speaking with the old fervor of the Infirmary days, she planned an organization which should have only one simple purpose, to teach people how to keep well!

She talked of the sicknesses that were preventable, of deaths that should never have occurred, of diseases that should never have been endured. She talked of the horrors she had seen at Blockley, of tenements where children slept three and four in a bed, and were brought up on bread and coffee.

Was it not true that children who slept in dark bedrooms, played without sunshine, ate poor and unvaried food, died more readily, succumbed sooner to diphtheria, scarlet fever, pneumonia; recovered more slowly from croup, measles, whooping cough and the other disorders of childhood?

She spoke of long working hours and of inadequate food; of houses without light; of consumption bred in cellars; of dirt, and neglect, and all the other causes of disease which, instead of being fated, were man-made.

Talking of physicians and their true responsibility, she said, "We are not tinkerers who simply patch and mend what is broken . . .

"We must be watchmen, guardians of the life and the health of our generation, so that stronger and more able generations may come after!"

She got together a staff of volunteer workers, and again with Kitty to help her, wrote letters and made pleas. A fund was raised, offices were rented, a permanent staff of secretaries was hired, and in 1871, in a suite of rooms on Berners Street, the new organization was established.

It was called the National Health Society, and had for its motto a sentence which Elizabeth had framed, "Prevention is Better Than Cure."

Through the schools, through churches, through speeches and editorials, this message of health, of disease prevention, was now enthusiastically carried forward. Branch organizations were founded, booklets were prepared, educational programs were planned and put into action.

"But the results will not be in our time," Elizabeth predicted. "This is an architecture of the future, for the benefit of generations to come!"

The ideas which she had shared with Florence Nightingale, in their Embley Park walks, which had seemed so vague and so distant then, had taken shape at last and were being translated into action.

Florence Nightingale, now directing her work from an invalid's bed, had talked in those days about her vision of great schools for training women in the intelligent and scientific care of the sick. In New York, Elizabeth had started at the Infirmary, the first school of nursing in America!

Now Elizabeth's own idea, a thought distilled from thirty years of practice—the thought that the masses of people could be taught to keep well—was taking practical shape. Inspired workers, Miss Toulmin Smith, the secretary of the National Health Society, and Miss Fay Lankester, the manager, took over Elizabeth's plans, plans which had been developed during the years of her tenement practice, and began with enthusiasm to put them into effect.

It was good to have such workers, for Elizabeth after a year of campaigning was very tired, was almost inclined to take the rest that she had for some time promised herself.

But a new project came up. One day a young woman, vivid with energy and full of enthusiasm, came to call on her. "I am one of your disciples!" she said.

More that a dozen years before, during her first visit to England, Elizabeth had given a series of talks on medicine as a career for women, at the Marylebone Literary Institute. Her caller was one of those who had been present.

"It changed my whole life!" she told Elizabeth, and went on to say that not only had she trained herself as a physician, but she was determined, as Elizabeth had done, to found a dispensary for women, perhaps a woman's college of medicine.

"What we want, of course," she said, "is your help!"

She identified herself as Dr. Elizabeth Garrett, adding

that one of Elizabeth's former students, Dr. Sophia Jex Blake, was working with her.

"We are planning to open a dispensary on Seymour Street," she said, "but with your name on the committee, with a person of your prestige as our speaker, we could do far more," she urged.

Elizabeth could not help promising. "But I can't give too much time," she said.

Her health had again been troublesome. Only the day before she had been on the point of telling Kitty that she was ready to cut off, ready to give up her practice, her work in London, ready to retire to the country, or travel as the doctors had urged her she must do.

"Just one push more," she now said to Kitty.

But as usual, once she had been drawn in, she had to go on. The old exuberance, the old excitement, if not the old vigor was there. Once more fund-raising, once more speeches into which she threw all of her energy, once more interviews, and attendance at the social affairs and the charities planned to raise money for the new institution.

At first the dispensary struggled, was too small, had too little money for the needs of the many patients who came flocking. Then there were some sick people who desperately needed more adequate care, good nursing, good food, attention that could only be given on the premises.

What was more natural than a new fund to start a hospital? And when the building had been rented and the beds installed, and the nurses and physicians selected, a new need occurred. Women students of medicine applied for permission to train in the wards.

The next step was a campaign to establish a recognized school of medicine for women—the first to be opened in England! The staff was chosen, the quarters secured, dissection facilities were arranged, and eminent surgeons and medical authorities were invited to participate. Elizabeth, in spite of her much impaired health now, for she was suffering again from attacks of biliary colic, sleepless nights, days of retching, accepted the post of lecturer.

Worn, more pale than before, in a severe black dress etched with a white ruching at the neck, her hair now altogether white, drawn back simply, she faced her first class, looked down at the comfortable, well-dressed young women in their crinolines who crowded the lecture room.

Were they serious? Did they know what the struggle meant? The practice of medicine, she warned, was now almost too easy for women. The great danger, now that women were accepted, she said, was that they might forget themselves as women!

"The true physician," she said, "must possess just those qualities most natural to women—tenderness, sympathy, guardianship.

"Remember that your patients are human beings—not cases!" The glib, cold attitude of the new generation of doctors, their concern with scientific facts only, was distasteful to her.

She spoke of her practice in the old tenement-house days, in the terrible Eleventh Ward in New York. "It requires faith and courage," she said, "to recognize the real human soul under the terrible mask of squalor and poverty. . . . The attitude of the student and doctor to the sick poor is a real test of the true physician!"

She spoke without notes, without reference to textbooks. The cases she had treated thirty years before were as vivid in her mind as the new cases to which she was called as consultant to survey in the wards.

She remembered her anxious, eager days at La Maternité, where she had concealed her medical training, had entered with the country girls as a student, so that she could be present in the wards of that famous hospital when the staff of surgeons with their following of internes made their calls.

How timidly she had edged toward the group by the bedside, hoping to catch a word, a sentence spoken by the consultant, standing on tiptoe to see how the diagnosis was made!

Now these young women had their own hospital, their own staff of surgeons to teach them. Could they appreciate, would they ever know the great value of what they were receiving?

She searched for talented students, and struggling with her own natural reserve, tried to pour into them something of what she was feeling. She was stern in her assignments, grim at the slightest weakness.

"You are trusted with human lives!" she said.

The drudgery of anatomy she made dramatic. In Dr. Allen's dissection rooms, under the hot slanting roof, during that summer in Philadelphia, before any medical school would accept her, she had come to know the awe and wonder of the human body. One could never study its structure long enough nor have a knowledge which was too profound.

She was not a genial, witty lecturer as Dr. Webster, the jolly little professor, had been. Her style was more serious, intense, her dignity impressive. The young women students stood in awe of her. Yet when they got up courage, came to see her in her office at the school, with their problems, she could be surprisingly gentle and kind, a little old lady with twinkling features and eyes of infinite wisdom under shrewd brows.

Her reputation, now almost world-wide, drew many students to the school, but her work, in spite of her great interest in it, she now found very taxing. One morning after a night of pain and gasping, a night of terror which showed her how serious her condition could be, she was unable to be present in the classroom, and she finished her lectures for the season with great difficulty.

In the spring she went abroad with Kitty, and would have

been unhappy even now at resting, except that such good news had been coming to her in recent months from New York. The Infirmary practice, Emily had written her, was growing. The out-patient department which Elizabeth had founded had been put in the hands of a recent graduate, a very talented young woman, Dr. Annie Daniels. Hundreds of patients were being taken care of in their homes by the visiting physician and her assistants, all trained to the ideal of teaching health habits and the prevention of further sickness.

This was a plan which Elizabeth had started, and flourishing now, it served as a model for other hospitals and institutions, for the idea of teaching people how to take care of themselves was beginning to gain recognition at last in the medical world.

The work which Elizabeth, years before, had visualized and begun, had taken root, was flourishing. More gratifying still to her was the news which came from Emily about the school, where more than two hundred women had been trained in the four-year course, and graduated, and were now practicing! How happy they had been in the opening year, right after the war with the South, to greet fifteen venturesome women—their first class.

In the long letters which she received from Emily, who acted as dean of the college, superintendent of the Infirmary, and director of the dispensary in New York, there was news also of their early collaborator, Dr. Zakrzewska.

Elizabeth remembered the eager German girl who had stood on her doorstep, saying that she must, that she would somehow become a physician.

Marie was now head of the New England Hospital for Women in Boston. And in the fine new buildings in which the hospital was housed, Emily reported, a most interesting new service had been opened, a department of home visitors and advisors, the first hospital social service in America!

The attitude toward women and their work in medicine had changed, her sister wrote to Elizabeth. In all parts of the country, the state legislatures now voted funds for institutions operated by women, for women. Distinguished citizens did not hesitate to serve as directors of these women's hospitals. And the old arguments about "the ladies who study medicine because they want to be men," were no longer heard.

Even the medical profession was no longer hostile. A woman, one of Elizabeth's early co-workers, Dr. Mary Putnam Jacobi, had been awarded the Boyleston prize for her research, and there was talk that she might even be appointed as clinical lecturer at a school of medicine attended by men!

"Any age of reforms," Elizabeth had once said, "is stirring!"

But stirring too, even though she could not now be so active, was the feeling of fulfillment that came to her as she read and heard of the steady growth and development of the work which had resulted from her early struggles.

Kitty kept up a voluminous correspondence for her. Together, under faintly-colored parasols, they strolled the beach at Nice, talking all the while of one student and another: Dr. Sophia Jex Blake in Edinburgh; Dr. Garrett in London, now head of the Women's Hospital and College; Dr. Jacobi in New York. The young women whom Elizabeth had taught, practicing in many of the big cities of America and the Continent, carrying forward the work she had started, made her feel less lonely now that she had fallen back, could not participate any longer in the struggle.

"I have faith," she had once said, "that having cast my bread upon the waters it has done its work!"

But the impulse to work persisted, the ferment of ideas, after the long years of action, would not cease. Sitting under the olive trees at Bordighera, by the lovely blue sea, she began to dictate to Kitty a new book. *Counsel for Parents,* this volume was called. And when it was completed, twelve prominent publishers of London were to reject it, one even saying that publication of the manuscript would "make her name a forbidden word in England!"

This aroused Elizabeth, who felt in her first hour of anger, all the old energy flowing back. She returned to London, and defiantly made arrangements to have the book printed privately, seeing to it herself that it was placed on a few selected bookstands.

The book at first caused no comment. Being paper-bound and inexpensively put out, it was not noticed. Then one day a young woman of liberal ideas, Miss Ellice Hopkins, known for her interest in social movements, happened to come upon a copy. She took it at once to Hatchard and Company, a very fine publishing house, and prevailed upon them to bring it out in a good edition.

"Such a work should not be neglected," she said.

The arrangements, since she was a person of influence, were made, the book was printed, and then suddenly, at the last moment, all the copies were withdrawn! A board member, widow of a bishop and a person of pious notions, had demanded the proofs, had read them, had thrown them into the fire, and had insisted that publication be stopped!

Upon receiving the news, Elizabeth, who was living quietly in a hillside cottage at Hastings, returned at once to the city. There she called together a committee of elderly and dignified clergymen.

"If there is anything reprehensible here," she said, asking them to examine the book, "then it's in the minds of those who read, and not in this manuscript!"

The committee withdrew, read the material that was submitted to them, and returned to give their verdict. By all means the volume was publishable, they said, and suggested only a slight change in title. The book appeared under a new name, *Moral Education for the Young*, and not only passed through a number of editions, but was translated many times into foreign languages. Like so many of Elizabeth's ideas which had seemed at first so revolutionary, it was finally accepted.

Elizabeth had been insistent, had fought harder for this book than for any other, because the theme was so important to her. "Children," she wrote, "must be well born, well nourished, well educated!" How such a notion could be thought bad she could hardly understand.

Strangely now, it was in France, where as a student she had had the least cooperation, that her work was accepted and welcomed. In 1889, a book telling the story of her life appeared in Paris. It was written by a French writer, E. M. Mesnard, and entitled *Miss Elizabeth Blackwell and the Women of Medicine*, it gave a sympathetic survey of all that she had accomplished.

Her early work, *The Religion of Health*, was translated into French, and writing to a friend about the translation, she said, "I rejoiced to welcome the little old friend. May it continue to do its tiny work for God and Humanity when I have disappeared from human eyes."

Her life was very quiet now. In "Rock House" at Hastings, she lived with Kitty, spent her mornings in writing, her afternoons in charity calls to the poor families of the town, in whose plight she was always interested.

Her sisters were near her. Marion, who once had said, "I'm never afraid when I'm near you," had come from America where she had remained after the death of her mother.

Anna, retiring at last from her journalistic work, had come from Paris. "I guess," she had written, "that I'll rusticate somewhere near you."

Marion looked incredibly frail, her hair completely white, her body shrunken. Only the Blackwell eyes, dark and piercing, were alive still, and her preoccupation with ideas, had not altered. She brought trunks of books, and to the cottage which she occupied at the side of Rock House came a flood of publications and journals.

Anna was sharp, eccentric, more individual than ever. Edgar Allen Poe had once written a favorable criticism of her first book of poetry, and as a woman of letters, a famous journalist, she considered herself an authority on all subjects.

Sometimes the three women talked of their brothers, both of whom had married famous suffragettes. Henry, so like their father in his zeal for movements, had worked side by side with his wife, Lucy Stone, founder of the American Women's Suffrage Association. With his wife and his daughter, Alice Stone Blackwell, he had for many years published a notable journal of feminism in Boston.

Once there had been a price on his head for aiding in the rescue of a slave girl. Now he exerted himself for the Jews of Russia, for persecuted people everywhere. As a small boy he had been called "curmudgeon" because he fought so readily against odds. He had been fighting against odds ever since for anyone, race, group, or people that needed helping. And his daughter Alice, tiny, bright, individual, was a fighter too, carrying on, since Lucy Stone's death, the tradition of her mother's work.

Like the childhood friend of their household, the great "Liberator" William Lloyd Garrison, Alice translated Russian poetry. She had learned to read Yiddish too, and Armenian, and wrote on the literatures of these strange languages.

Marion, reporting on her work, for she had most recently been in America, had to comment that the "Blackwell women always had to set out on strange paths!"

Elizabeth's "companion brother" Samuel, who had married Antoinette Brown, the minister, had participated with his wife too, in her pioneer work. She had been a prominent lecturer, had written books well received in America. They had five daughters. Of these, two were physicians, both having been trained by Emily at the Infirmary school. The liberal tradition persisted.

Anna and Marion talked often of the past. But Elizabeth was too energetic to be interested for long in anything but current movements. Her correspondence was tremendous. And writing, revising, editing, she prepared continually new editions of her published works for which there was now a great demand.

Of the three sisters, Elizabeth now as always was still the most vital. Going down to the village with Kitty, she would turn around suddenly. "I guess I'll run up the hill to see what the girls are doing!"

Sometimes Marion was ill, sometimes Anna. She would doctor them both in turn, grumbling all the while that they were more trouble than a whole dispensary full of patients. But the old authority was there, the power to hold a patient persisted. It was Marion who complained that she could not die until Elizabeth would let her!

And now the years, passing rapidly, seemed to flow one into the other. Great events were taking place in the world outside, but the echo of their excitement seemed to the old women on the hill to be dim and distant. The Boer War had been fought and forgotten. Bustles had come, been disapproved, and gave way to mannish waists and skirts, trim but audacious hats. The Queen's Jubilee Year was approaching, and for Elizabeth, too, despite her withdrawal, her now monotonously quiet life in the English town, had come great honors . . .

On the campus of Geneva College (now called Hobart College), the fiftieth anniversary of her graduation was being celebrated. Fifty years—how long ago it seemed, how distant! A college for women had been endowed, and the first dormitory was being named Elizabeth Blackwell House, in her honor!

A letter of congratulations had come from the president of the college. She held it in her hands . . . Her thoughts were slipping into the past again . . . were with a young girl, slight, blond, almost lost in a full Quaker-like gown, a deep old-fashioned bonnet. She saw the white cupola of the school, and the blue of the lake below it, and felt the cold silence like a blow which had greeted her on first entering the classroom.

She remembered the music of the processional the organist had played as the students had marched into the church, and she remembered turning to the president as he sat on the platform. "Sir," she could hear herself saying, "I thank you; by the help of the Most High it shall be the effort of my life to shed honor upon your diploma."

Could it be possible, fifty years . . . a whole lifetime . . . it seemed now to be unreeling behind her, all the scenes merging together: the wards at Blockley, gray and dim under the night lamps; La Maternité and her long illness; the gift to M. Blot; hurrying weak and shaken down the long, cold, echoing corridors; the long watches in tenement rooms at night in New York, and she was begging, pleading, arguing for the money with which to build up the hospital, the hospital from which Emily had written her, that she was retiring, at last.

She passed her hand over her forehead, as if to stop the race of memories, and heard Kitty's voice speaking to her.

"The college is very proud of the fact that you are a graduate of it . . ." Kitty had taken the letter from Elizabeth's hand and was reading it to her. "And in naming the first dormitory of the co-education school in memory of you, we have given not only satisfaction to ourselves, but distinction to the college!

"We have invited Miss Alice Stone Blackwell, your niece,

and your sister Miss Emily Blackwell to be with us. We wish that you might be with us too. Will you not receive from me and from the authorities of the college our profound felicitations upon your useful and noble career . . ."

So Henry's daughter, bright, bird-like little Alice, who had turned out a suffragette, a leader of women like her mother, Lucy Stone, was going to be there; and Emily, to whom the college had refused admission, whom they would not receive as a student even after Elizabeth had been successfully graduated.

Fifty years . . . it seemed hardly believable. The buildings must have changed . . . and the people . . . Dr. Webster, the jolly little anatomy professor, was gone. Dr. Lee, so kind at heart, yet so fearful of the good name, the decorum of the school, had vanished. The people of the town who had stared at her, who had made her first months in Geneva so miserable, that even now she could remember the pain, were gone too . . . figures of dust, a dream, a mirage, all melted away.

Elizabeth, with her hands in her lap, looked down. Life, a river, flowing away. And now the tide of her own life, so rapidly ebbing, like sand dropping away.

She was incredibly frail now, sitting whole days at the window to look out on the valley, where every shade on the grass, every shadow, seemed more alive, more fragrant.

"How lovely the outburst of spring foliage is!" she wrote to her old friend Mrs. Browne. "I look up my valley, and see the horse chestnuts, the sycamores, and every bush and tree seems to me more beautiful than I ever have seen it."

It seemed to her she was imbued now with a sharper sense of living than ever before. There was the richness, the fullness of work well completed; the satisfaction of being well acquitted of the task that, in the distant past, she had begun. Her medical writings, once thought so revolutionary, were accepted everywhere, translated into many languages, working their influence with clarity on the new generations

—who listened and understood better than those for whom the books in the first instance had been written.

Her last book, *Pioneer Work for Women,* an autobiography shaped from her diaries and letters, had passed through many editions, and constantly letters came to her from young physicians everywhere.

"You have shown the way," wrote one woman doctor after reading the book, "and we are accordingly moving on to more and more light."

And from another woman engaged in the practice of medicine had come a letter fully bridging the distance from one generation to another. "If the young people would only put a little of the moral qualities into their work that you put into yours when you set out on your lonely way," this writer exclaimed.

The way was not lonely any longer. Elizabeth sat down to answer the letter but could not find words. Instead, she found herself writing to an old friend who had written to her recently, reproaching her for still continuing with her work.

"Each soul," she wrote now to this friend, "must answer to its Maker, so I work on in joyful faith!"

And in truth she was working still, working in the lives of others, for the river of her own life was enlarged now into a sea encompassing many lives, with a tide which was full and vigorous, even though she herself felt small, frail, almost engulfed.

Still there was a core, a little warm ember of life that persisted. She asked Kitty to take her back once more to Kilmun, in Scotland, where on a beautiful winding arm of the sea, during the later less eventful years of her life, she had spent so many happy summers.

She had told Kitty one evening that there were just two places where she would like to think of herself as resting: beautiful Campo Santo of Genoa, and Kilmun, on Holy Loch, where the sound of the waves was forever reverberating, and the mists dropping down made sky and land melt as if into a cloud.

In the rooms of the old-fashioned inn at Kilmun, she would sit whole afternoons long, while Kitty read to her and answered letters which she had forgotten, or else watched while Elizabeth dozed, awoke, and slept again.

One May morning, for May had always been the month of great events for her, she dozed in her chair. Then, with a deepening, sinking tranquillity, she drew an almost imperceptible breath, and, her head nodding forward ever so gently, she passed into a deeper sleep.

She lies in the hamlet of Kilmun, in the old-fashioned churchyard where she had walked so many evenings with Kitty.

On a plain Celtic cross, behind the mausoleum of Douglass of Glenfennert, and not far from that of the Argyll family, on the almost severe, bare stone, standing a little away from the others, is written her history.

"In loving memory of Elizabeth Blackwell, M.D.—born at Bristol, 3rd February, 1821, died at Hastings, 31st May, 1910. The first woman of modern times to graduate in medicine (1849) and the first to be placed on the British Medical Register (1859)."

Underneath is a line from Elizabeth's lecture on *The Religion of Health*, always her favorite work.

"It is only when we have learned to recognize that God's law for the human body is as sacred as—nay, is one with—God's law for the human soul, that we shall begin to understand the religion of the heart."

A few months later, Emily, who in everything had followed Elizabeth, was laid to rest, too.

The pioneer work was over. . . .